PERSONAL ADVENTURES DURING THE INDIAN REBELLION IN ROHILCUND, FUTTEHGHUR, AND OUDE

PERSONAL ADVENTURES DURING THE INDIAN REBELLION IN ROHILCUND, FUTTEHGHUR, AND OUDE

WILLIAM EDWARDS

Published by

FacsiMile Publisher
12 Pragati Market
Ashok Vihar, Ph-2
Delhi - 110052, India
Phone: 011-47034999
Email: www.facsimilepublishers.com
info@facsimilepublishers.com

Distribution Network
gyanbooks.com
India, USA, Canada, UK, Australia

ISBN: 978-93-3347-278-4 (PB)
First Published, 1858

2nd Impression 2026

Printed at: Gyan Press, Delhi.

PERSONAL ADVENTURES DURING THE INDIAN REBELLION IN ROHILCUND, FUTTEHGHUR, AND OUDE
Author: WILLIAM EDWARDS

PERSONAL ADVENTURES

DURING THE

INDIAN REBELLION

IN

ROHILCUND, FUTTEHGHUR, AND OUDE.

BY WILLIAM EDWARDS, ESQ., B.C.S.,

JUDGE OF BENARES, AND LATE MAGISTRATE AND COLLECTOR
OF BUDAON IN ROHILCUND.

THIRD EDITION, REVISED.

LONDON:
SMITH, ELDER AND CO., 65, CORNHILL.

1858.

PREFACE.

The following Narrative, drawn up as opportunity offered, under circumstances of great personal danger and considerable anxiety, was transmitted to my family in England, the day after I had providentially succeeded with my companions in escaping into Cawnpore, and joining the force under the late General Havelock. From that time until April last, when, from the failure of my health, I was forced to leave India, I had no opportunity of reverting to the subject of my escape.

Since my return, last month, I have had leisure to look the Diary over, and have been induced to offer it for publication, under the impression that, at a time like the present, when public attention is so much occupied with the Indian Rebellion, the events it relates, although of a purely personal nature, may not be without interest.

W. EDWARDS,

Bengal Civil Service,

Judge of Benares.

June 24, 1858.

PERSONAL ADVENTURES

DURING THE

INDIAN REBELLION IN ROHILCUND, FUTTEHGHUR, AND OUDE.

KUSSOURAH, LEFT BANK OF THE RAMGUNGAH, ABOUT TWELVE MILES N.E. OF FUTTEHGHUR, JULY 27TH, 1857.

THIS day, for the first time since the first of June, I have writing materials at my disposal. I shall therefore endeavour to record, as correctly as I can from memory, a narrative of the events that have occurred to me since that sad day, the first of June, when it pleased God that I should become a wanderer and a fugitive. I must premise that shortly after the outbreak and massacre at Meerut, about the 19th May, so far as I can recollect, the spirit of disorder began to show itself in the Budaon district in Rohilcund, of which I was Magistrate and Collector—the infection having spread from the tracts on the right bank of the Ganges, which were by that time in open rebellion. Bands of marauders sprang up, as it were by magic, and commenced plundering on the roads, and sacking and burning villages.

I became alarmed for the safety of my wife and child, and despatched them to a place of security, Nynee Tal, which station they reached safely; but they did not start one moment too soon, for they passed through Bareilly, after that station had been deserted by all the European ladies and children, and just the day week before the mutiny and massacre occurred there. Since the 28th of May I have heard nothing of them, and it is now very doubtful whether I may ever do so, or see them again in this world.

As soon as the disturbance began I doubled the police force in my district, horse and foot, on my own responsibility; but notwithstanding my endeavours to maintain the peace, the disorders daily increased. In the Etah district across the Ganges, immediately opposite to Budaon, they had reached a most alarming height; all our communications had been cut off with Agra, Calcutta, and the South; the runners being unable to convey the mails along the chief lines of road. In the district of Moradabad, immediately adjoining Budaon to the north, the sepoys of the regiment broke open the jail and let out a great number of the prisoners.

I was informed of this fact by a short note from Campbell, the joint magistrate, telling me to look out for myself, as among the liberated convicts, was a notorious villain, Nujjoo Khan*, who was under sentence of transportation for life for an attempt to murder Court, joint magistrate of Budaon, and in which he very nearly succeeded, having maimed him for life. I had succeeded in apprehending this miscreant, who had eluded our police force for more than two years, and in bringing him to justice; he was consequently highly exasperated with me, and, as Campbell informed me, had started at once towards my station with the intention of murdering me.

This intelligence did not tend much to improve my position, which already was by no means a pleasant one. I was the sole European officer in charge of the district, with a lawless population of nearly 1,100,000 souls. The entire

* Nujjoo Khan has since become a rebel leader of note, and his capture has just been reported by the force now at Moradabad in Rohilcund under Brigadier Jones.

management and responsibility rested on me; for my sole assistant was a Mohammedan deputy-collector, who only joined the station early in the month, and I could, of course, devolve no duty upon him. The nearest European officers were at Bareilly, some thirty miles distant from Budaon.

On Monday, the 25th of May, I received certain information that the Mohammedans of the town of Budaon, who were on that day assembled for prayers on occasion of the Ede festival, were to rise at noon and create a riot, which would probably have resulted in the plunder and destruction of the place. I at once summoned the most influential inhabitants of that persuasion to meet me at my house. They immediately came, many of them very fierce and insolent, and all in a most excited state. Soon after they were seated and I had commenced talking with them, I saw Wuzeer Singh, a Sikh peon, and one of my personal guards, come up quietly behind me, with my revolver in his belt and my gun in his hand, and station himself immediately behind my chair. In the tumult and excitement, and where all were armed, his entrance was unnoticed, but his quiet and determined demeanour made me for the first time feel an assurance that he was a man I could depend upon in any difficulty or danger. This Wuzeer Singh, whose tried fidelity, courage, and devotion make me regard him as Paul did Onesimus, "not now so much as a servant as a brother beloved," deserves some notice from me here.

He is an inhabitant of Nowserah near Umritzur in the Punjaub, and was originally a sepoy, belonging to the Sikh company of the 29th Regiment of N. I. (the corps which mutinied at Shajehanpore, and murdered all its officers and all the Europeans in the Church at that place). While on detachment duty at Saharunpore, some years previous, he was converted to Christianity by the Protestant Missionaries at that place; but was never baptized.* In December, 1856, he came to Budaon from Shahjehanpore, where his regiment was quartered, with the rest of his company, to form the guard over my treasury. There happened to be several native Christians at Budaon, and he attended service with them every Sunday at my house. When the detachment was relieved, and returned to head-quarters in April 1857, Wuzeer Singh,

* Wuzeer Singh was baptized at Benares on the 16th of last March by the Rev. James Kennedy. He has received a life pension from the Government of India for his faithful services during the rebellion.

wishing to join himself to this company of Christians, retired from the regiment, and came back to Budaon early in May, when I gave him service as an orderly on my personal guard as magistrate; he was therefore only a few days with me before the occurrences to which I have alluded took place, at the Ede Festival. His devotion then and subsequently, therefore, does him the more honour, springing as it did from a sense of duty to his immediate superior, and not from any feelings of attachment to a master after a service extending over a long period of time.

To return to my visitors. By degrees they calmed down, and by leading them into conversation, and reasoning with them, and above all playing off one party against another—knowing as I did that a bitter animosity existed between several of them—I managed to occupy their attention until the time fixed for the rising had passed. The plots, which I do not doubt were premeditated, were for the time defeated, and the day, to my infinite relief (ah, what a long one it was!) passed off quietly. I think I never wished more in my life for some one of my own countrymen to talk to, than during these miserable days between the 20th and 27th of May. I had every reason to distrust the sepoys forming my Treasury Guard, who belonged to the 68th Regiment N. I., at Bareilly; and it was by no means comfortable to sit in the close vicinity of these gentlemen, who at any moment might break out into open mutiny and murder me. My police were little more to be depended on, and I felt my isolation greatly. It was, therefore, with no small joy, that while sitting at my solitary dinner on the 27th May, I saw my cousin Alfred Phillipps, magistrate of Etah, ride up to the house, escorted by about a dozen horsemen, some belonging to different regiments of irregular horse, others common police sowars.

He gave a most deplorable account of the state of things in his district, and had himself, with his men, had an affair with a body of rebels in the town of Khasgunj, in which he killed no less than three men with his own hand. He had come across the Ganges, with the view of going to Bareilly to procure some military aid to put down the disturbances, I was forced to disabuse him of this hope, informing him that I had already myself more than once applied for aid in vain, as none could be spared.

Up to the 30th, matters went on from bad to worse, the disorder being considerably aggravated by the impossibility of my leaving the station to proceed to the immediate scene of disturbance, as I had no officer to whom I could make over charge of the treasury. On the afternoon of Saturday the 30th, I learnt that the important town of Bhilsea was about to be attacked by the rebels, and I at once sent off an express to the comissioner at Bareilly, entreating him to send me some aid; as my police, the old establishment as well as the new levies, were quite unable to meet the crisis, or at all events would not exert themselves.

On Sunday, May 31st, I assembled, for the last time probably on earth, my little congregation at Budaon. Just as I closed the Hindustani service in the afternoon, a man rushed in with a note from Etah for Phillipps, written by one of his native officers, saying that Bramley, the joint magistrate of Futtehghur, was to be at Puttealee, the head-quarters of the Etah district, the next day, with two regiments to restore the peace.

We were both overjoyed at this intelligence and were full of plans, how Phillipps should first punish the rebels in his district, and then come over to aid me, in setting mine in order.

Shortly after, about 9 P.M., I received from the Commissioner an express, in reply to my earnest appeal for aid, informing me that a company of native infantry, under a European officer, was to start on that day from Bareilly to my assistance. I immediately took measures for sending out carts to bring in the men the last half of the way, so that they might be moved at once to Bhilsea, the point threatened; and thus arrive there fresh and unfatigued. I next sent off a horseman with a note to the commanding officer of the detachment informing him of these arrangements, and begging him to press on as speedily as possible. I then retired to rest, happy and thankful. Phillipps, equally happy in the prospect of having assistance suited to the emergency, was to start at three in the morning to return to Etah.

About half-past two I got up in order to wake him, when just as I was leaving my room, a chuprassee rushed up to me, saying that the horseman I had sent off to meet the detachment had just returned with the terrible intelligence that the road from Bareilly up to within eight miles of Budaon was covered with convicts escaped from gaol—the sepoys forming the Bareilly garrison having on Sunday forenoon broken out into open mutiny, massacred the Europeans, fired the station, and broken open the great central gaol, which contained nearly four thousand of the most desperate characters in India. He further stated that a detachment of the mutineers were in full march to Budaon, to join the Treasury Guard there, and plunder and burn the station. This was indeed terrible news, and the excited manner of the sowar and the condition of his panting horse, showed that the tale was too true, and that he had ridden for his life to give me the intelligence.

I at once woke up Phillipps and communicated to him the disastrous intelligence. He called for his horse and followers, and in ten minutes after dashed off at full gallop, in order to get to the Ghauts across the Ganges before the convicts or mutineers could reach it and prevent his return to the scene of his duty. I most bitterly regret that I did not follow his example, and thus make my escape from Budaon, where I could do no good, and endeavour to reach the hills, which I then might have succeeded in doing. I thought it, however, my duty not to desert my post, but stick to the ship as long as she floated. I went into my room and prayed earnestly that God would protect and guide me, and enable me to do my duty. I then summoned my kotwal, and arranged with him as best we could, for maintaining as long as possible the peace and the safety of the town. My great object was to prevent the gangs of escaped convicts, the most desperate characters in the country, from entering the place; and in this I was happily successful. It was, however, quite hopeless to expect to defend the station against the mutineers; who, on their arrival, would be at once joined by the 100 men forming the Treasury Guard. I could therefore only hope, and it scarcely amounted to a hope, to keep things quiet until the mutineers might arrive from Bareilly.

About 10 A.M., I was joined by Mr. Donald and Son, indigo planters in the district; who, having had their lives threatened at their residence in Ooghannee, had come into the station for protection. Mr. Gibson, a patrol in the Customs Department—temporarily on duty in the interior of the district, also sought safety in my house—as did Mr. Stewart, one of my clerks, with his wife and family. They were under the impression that

I could protect them, whereas the fact was, that the number of Europeans congregated together, by atttracting attention, seriously increased our mutual danger, and at the same time greatly impeded my movements.

I was satisfied that as long as I was alone I could provide for my own safety, having numbers of friends in the district able and anxious to protect and shelter me; but they were unwilling in any way to compromise their own safety by granting an asylum to the others: more especially as some of the party were at feud with the people of the district, in consequence of having purchased estates, sold under harsh circumstances, by decrees of our Civil Courts.

To the large number of these sales during the past twelve or fifteen years, and the operation of our revenue system, which has had the result of destroying the gentry of the country and breaking up the village communities, I attribute solely the disorganization of this and the neighbouring districts in these provinces.

By fraud or chicanery, a vast number of the estates of families of rank and influence have been alienated, either wholly or in part, and have been purchased by new men—chiefly traders or Government officials—without character or influence over their tenantry. These men, in a vast majority of instances, were also absentees, fearing or disliking to reside on their purchases, where they were looked upon as interlopers and unwelcome intruders. The ancient proprietary of these alienated estates were again living as tenantry on the lands once theirs; by no means reconciled to their change of position, but maintaining their hereditary hold as strong as ever over the sympathies and affections of the agricultural body, who were ready and willing to join their feudal superiors in any attempt to recover their lost position and regain possession of their estates. The ancient landed proprietary body of the Budaon district were thus still in existence, but in the possession of tenants, not proprietors. None of the men who had succeeded them as landowners were possessed of sufficient influence or power to give me any aid in maintaining the public tranquillity. On the contrary, the very first people who came in to me, imploring aid, were this new proprietary body, to whom I had a right to look for vigorous and efficient efforts in the maintenance of order. On the other hand, those who really could control the vast masses of the rural population were interested in bringing about a state of disturbance and general anarchy.

For more than a year previous to the outbreak, I had been publicly representing to superior authority the great abuse of the power of the civil courts, and the reckless manner in which they decreed the sale of rights and interests connected with the soil, in satisfaction of petty debts, and the dangerous dislocation of society which was in consequence being produced. I then pointed out that although the old families were being displaced fast, we could not destroy the memory of the past, or dissolve the ancient connection between them and their people; and I said distinctly, that in event of any insurrection occurring, we should find this great and influential body, through whom we can alone hope to control and keep under the millions forming the rural classes, ranged against us on the side of the enemy, with their hereditary retainers and followers rallying around them, in spite of our attempts to separate their interests. My warnings were unheeded; and I was treated as an alarmist, who, having hitherto only served in the political department of the State, and being totally inexperienced in revenue matters, could give no sound opinion on the subject. Little did I think at the time, that my fears and forebodings were so soon to be realized.

The leaders and promoters of this great rebellion, whoever they may have been, knew well the inflammable condition, from these causes, of the rural society in the North-Western Provinces, and they therefore sent among them the chupaties, as a kind of fiery cross, to call them to action. These cakes passed with the most amazing rapidity over the length and breadth of the land. Where they came from originally it is impossible to say, but I believe Barrackpore was the starting point, where large masses of mutinous sepoys were congregated. The chupaties entered my district from the adjoining one of Shajehanpore; a village watchman of that place giving to the watchman of the nearest Budaon village two of the cakes, with an injunction to make six fresh ones, retain two for his own, and give the others to the watchman of the next village, who would follow the same course, and continue the manufacture and distribution. I truly believe that the rural population of all classes, among whom these cakes spread, were as ignorant as I was myself of their real object; but it was clear they were a secret sign to be on the alert, and the minds of the people were through them kept watchful and excited. As soon as the disturbances broke out at Meerut and Delhi, the cakes explained themselves, and the people at once perceived what was expected of them.

In Budaon the mass of the population rose in a body, and the entire district became a scene of anarchy and confusion. The ancient proprietary body took the opportunity of murdering or expelling the auction purchasers, and resumed possession of their hereditary estates. The danger now is, that this vast mass of our subjects, who are numbered by tens of thousands, and who are the real thews and sinews of the country, will never consent to the restoration of a Government to power which they consider treated them with harshness; whose system tended to depress and dispossess them, and whose first measures after the return of tranquillity they consider must be to put back the auction purchasers and evict them. I feel convinced that no amount of force will restore us to power, unless at the same time some measures be taken for undoing the evils of the past, and coming to some compromise, by which the old families may be reinstated, and their sympathies and interests enlisted on our behalf, while those of the auction purchasers are also duly cared for. I am fully satisfied that the rural classes would never have joined in rebelling with the sepoys, whom they hated, had not these causes of discontent already existed. They evinced no sympathy whatever about the cartridges, or flour said to be made of human bones, and could not then have been acted upon by any cry of their religion being in danger. It is questions involving their rights and interests in the soil and hereditary holdings, invariably termed by them as "jan see azeez," "*dearer than life*," which excite them to a dangerous degree.

To return to my narrative of events on the fatal 1st of June. About noon, I collected all my guests into the drawing-room, and we all joined in hearty prayers to God for his mercy and protection in our desperate circumstances. I trust that we were heard; but what has been the fate of all those present, except myself and Mr. Gibson, I know not. I then earnestly advised the two Donalds, Mr. Gibson, and the Stewarts, to leave me and make for the hills, while there was yet time, pointing out that our safety was far more endangered by remaining together and attracting attention than by separating. My own duty was clear, to remain at my post as long as any semblance of order could be maintained; they were under no such obligation, and had only to consult their own safety. All my arguments and entreaties, however, were in vain. They were quite paralysed, and seemed to feel that their only hope was in sticking close to the magistrate for protection. The day, which was a very hot one, wore on most gloomily. Every moment reports of one complexion or another were being brought to me of risings in the town, the defection of individuals in the police, and of the near approach of a large body of mutineers from Bareilly to murder me, plunder the treasury, and break open the jail.

About 4 P.M., the native officer of the sepoy guard over the treasury, composed of one hundred men of the 68th Native Infantry, which corps had mutinied at Bareilly the previous day, came to report all right. I took him aside, and inquired the real state of affairs. He denied, with the most solemn oaths any person of his persuasion could take, all knowledge of the Bareilly mutiny; asserting that no intimation had come to the guard from their comrades at Bareilly, and that, as long as Colonel Troup lived, he was confident the regiment would remain loyal. He then informed me that the guard were much alarmed in consequence of the excited state of the town, fearing they might be attacked by overwhelming numbers of budmashes, who would then sack the treasury, and he begged me earnestly to come down and join the guard, who would thereby be quite reassured. The man's earnest and respectful manner quite deceived me: I thought, if ever any one spoke truth it is this person. I at once, therefore, expressed my willingness to go, and told him to start, and I would follow presently. I then ordered my buggy, and was about stepping into it to drive off, when Wuzeer Singh came and implored me not to go, saying he knew these fellows well and that they meant mischief. I took his advice, and sent off my buggy.

I regard this incident with deep thankfulness, as one of the many marked interpositions of Almighty care in preserving my life, which have occurred within the past two months. Had I placed myself in the hands of the guard, they would immediately have murdered me; for I subsequently ascertained that a messenger from the regiment at Bareilly had reached the guard about four in the morning, to inform them of what had occurred there, and prepare them for the advance of a body of mutineers to Budaon in the evening. The guard waited for my expected arrival at the kutcherry for above an hour and a half, and then finding that I was not coming, they would be restrained no longer, but broke out into open mutiny. A party of them might easily have been sent to my house to seize and destroy me, but not a man would consent to leave the immediate neighbourhood of the Treasury, lest the plundering should commence in their absence, and they should lose their share of the spoil.

Their first act was to break open the gaol, distant about 100 yards from the Treasury, and release some 300 prisoners who were confined within. A tumultuous noise and shouting about 6 P.M. announced to me that the work of destruction had begun; at the same moment information was brought me that the mutineers from Bareilly were entering the station, and that all my police had thrown away their badges and joined them. The released prisoners then came shouting and yelling close up to my house. I felt my work was then over; that the ship had sunk under me, and that it was now time to try and provide for my own safety. My horse, a small grey Cabul galloway belonging to my wife and constantly ridden by her, on whose speed and endurance I knew I could depend, had been standing all day saddled; I at once mounted him, and rode slowly away from the house, followed by the Messrs Donald and Gibson.

The town, then full of mutineers, lay between us and the road to Moradabad, by which I had hoped to escape to the hills; I was therefore anxious to give the mutineers time to get to the Treasury, which I knew would be their first point, and then endeavour to make a circuit round and thus fall into the Moradabad road. When I had gone some hundred yards from the house I was met by the chief of Shikooporah, a Mohammedan gentleman of family and influence, who used frequently to visit me. He dissuaded me from attempting to get round the town, as the roads were crowded with sepoys and released convicts. He begged me to come and take refuge in his house, about three miles off, and in a different direction from that I had intended taking. This I readily consented to do, as I hoped that I could remain concealed with him until the mutineers had abandoned the station; when I would have returned, and endeavoured to resume my duties and restore some degree of order. The sheikh at the same time said he would grant an asylum to me alone, but not to the others of my party. I, however, thought I might be able to induce him to abandon this resolution, and retain us all, and I therefore took no notice at the time. We then turned and accompanied the sheikh. We had to return past my house, and, though scarcely ten minutes had elapsed since leaving it, I found the work of plundering it had already commenced, and that my own chuprassees were busily employed appropriating my property. The first man I saw was one of my own orderlies, and who had been a favourite of mine, with my dress-sword on him. Of course I was in no position to resent his conduct, or even notice it.

I was now obliged to leave poor Mr. Stewart, my clerk and his family. They were in sad distress, for they had neglected my warning in the morning to effect their escape while it was possible, and now it was apparently too late; their only conveyance being a buggy which could proceed only by regular roads, and these were all blocked up by the mutineers and rebels. There was nothing for them but to hide in the fields; and all I could do for them, in my own desperate circumstances, was to consign them to the care of an influential man in the city who had just come up to see how it fared with me. He promised to look after them, and I hope has done so; what has become of them, however, I know not, but as they were East Indians and nearly as dark as the natives, I trust they managed to escape, and are now alive.

My heart was indeed heavy in finally leaving that peaceful happy home, where, for the past eighteen months, we had enjoyed much rational happiness and blessed tranquillity. When I look back to that time in my present circumstances of peril, it appears like the days of heaven upon the earth. One of my private servants, an Afghan named Sooltan Mahommed Khan, accompanied me, and also Wuzeer Singh; who alone, of all the public establishment at Budaon, remained faithful to his salt. I had with me one change of clothes, which I entrusted to my groom; but he disappeared immediately, and I never saw him again, so I was reduced to those on my back. I took with me also a little Testament, and darling May's purse, intended for my birthday presents, and which had just reached me from home: these, with my watch and revolver, and 150 rupees divided between Sooltan Mahomed and Wuzeer Singh, who carried them round their waists, were all the worldly goods I possessed; and with them I went forth for the first time in my life without a home or a roof to cover me, and, like the patriarch, not knowing whither I went.

We waded the Yar Wuffardar river, which ran just below my house; and, after about an hour's riding, reached Shikooporah, without notice or molestation. Scarcely had we dismounted from our horses and entered the walled court, than one of the sheikh's brothers came up to me, and respectfully stated that it would be impossible for us to remain with safety there, as our numbers would certainly attract attention, and bring down upon us the mutineers; we must therefore at once leave, and go on to a village of his, about eighteen miles distant on the left bank of the Ganges. I was deeply mortified at this, and the consequent frustration of my hope of being able to lie close until the mutineers should decamp, and then return to the station. I therefore remonstrated strongly with the chief on his want of hospitality; but he remained quite firm, assuring me that while he was quite ready to shelter me alone, he would not grant an asylum to my companions. As they would not leave me, and I would not desert them, there was nothing for it but to comply with the sheikh's wishes, and start for the village further on. Fortunate it was for me that I did so.

I humbly regard this as another marked interposition of a merciful God to save my life; for shortly after we left Shikooporah, a body of Irregular Horse, who had accompanied the infantry portion of the mutineers from Bareilly (an event wholly unexpected by me, as the corps to which they belonged was considered staunch and loyal), beat up my temporary hiding place, and would have assuredly murdered me had they found me there, as they expected.

Kussowrah, 28th July.

I resume my writing, but with a lighter heart; for this morning, blessed be God, I have received tidings on which I can depend (the first since the 25th of May) of the safety of my beloved wife and child at Nynee Tal. Information was brought to me in the morning by some of the people in this village, (in which we are now living, under the protection of Hurdeo Buksh, an influential zemindar of Oude), that a stranger had arrived in the night and was making inquiries for me. He was suspected to be a spy from the rebels at Futtehghur or elsewhere, and his movements were being closely watched. I told my informant that I thought no harm could come of this man being brought before me. He was accordingly summoned, and turned out to be a common Kahar, or palkee bearer. I was in native dress, and he did not seem at first to recognise me; but at last said, "You are the sahib I have often seen in kutcherry at Budaon. I am a servant of Missur Byjenath's, the Bareilly banker, and he has sent me to ascertain if the report which had reached him that you were alive, and in hiding, is true, and to inform you (if I could find you) that the 'mem sahib' and the child are both well at Nynee Tal, and quite safe, and want for nothing, as my master has taken care to have them supplied with necessary funds." Oh, what a load was lifted off my heart, by the tidings.

This is the first messenger who has reached us from the outer world since the 13th of June. He informs me that poor Mr. Stewart, my clerk, and his family, are as yet safe and in hiding near

Budaon; that Khan Bahadhur Khan is in power at Bareilly, and has assumed the Government of Rohilcund; that poor Hay, Robertson, and Raikes, were among those massacred at Bareilly on the 31st of May; and that he had himself seen their dead bodies dragged through the city; but that several Europeans had escaped to Nynee Tal, among them the Commissioner Alexander and Colonel Troup.

The messenger, whose name was Khan Singh, had been ten days coming from Bareilly, owing to the inundations, the rains being peculiarly heavy—a most fortunate thing for us, as it prevents bands of mutineers and rebels wandering about the country. He informs us that our troops are at Delhi, and all is going on well there; that there is daily fighting, and that Agra and Meerut are still safe. Khan Singh wished at once to return to his master with the news respecting me, and I gave him a little letter, enclosed in a quill, for my wife, which he promised to convey safely to Nynee Tal. I have great hopes that he will be able to do so, as the piece of quill is not an inch long, and can be easily hidden in the mouth in case of challenge. He left us on his return in the evening.

I must now resume the narrative of my proceedings on the night of 1st June, after leaving Shikooporah. We were accompanied by one of the sheikhs, and travelled through by-ways and fields, leaving the high road at some distance to our left, in case of pursuit. We passed through a number of villages, literally swarming with men armed with swords and iron bound lathees. They were silent and not disrespectful, seeing us accompanied by the sheikh, whose tenantry they all were. He was, however, obliged to take the precaution to send men ahead to each village as we approached it, to prepare the people for our coming, and prevent any attack upon us. As we travelled on I looked back and saw a bright gleam of light in the sky, which I knew full well was from the burning bungalows in poor Budaon; all the property I possessed adding to the blaze.

We reached our destination about 12 P.M. It was a miserable village called Kukorah, but containing one better sort of house, in which the sheikh resided when he visited the place on business. We were sent up to the roof of this house, to pass the night; and there commenced my sleeping in the open air, which, with one or two exceptions, I have been forced to do ever since.

Before going to rest we all joined in prayer, thanking God for having so mercifully preserved us hitherto, and commending ourselves to His merciful protection for the future. Although weary and worn out with the events of the past 24 hours, I scarcely closed an eye. About 4 A.M. we were awoke by order of the sheikh, who recommended, indeed insisted, on our at once crossing the Ganges, to a place called Kadirchonk in the Etah district, where we would be, he declared, quite safe; which we could not hope to be much longer in his village, as the Irregular Cavalry would soon be on our track. I consented, thinking that by joining Phillipps and Bramley at Puttealee, I might get aid from them, and return to Budaon, to attempt to restore order. I was, however, doomed to bitter disappointment, as the sequel will show.

We took leave of the sheikh about 5 A.M., and rode to the bank of the Ganges, where we found a boat and crossed to the opposite side. The right bank was lined with a large concourse of people, assembled to attack and plunder some neighbouring village.* The crowd

* These assemblages of several villages to attack some large one the people call "Pukars," and it is quite astonishing

hailed us, and fired two or three shots at the boat, as we went down the centre of the stream; but the balls never came near us, and did no harm. We landed unmolested about a mile below this mob, and rode on to Kadir Chouk, a ruinous old fort, about two miles inland. The owner, a Mahomedan gentleman of some influence, received us very kindly, and assigned us a room, where we were sheltered from the heat, by this time become intense. His retainers, fully armed, were all assembled about the premises for the protection of the place, as a large body of marauders were assembled in the neighbourhood—others than those we saw on the river bank—and threatening an attack. At this time, as far as I could judge, this man was very well affected towards our Government, and was in high spirits; information having just reached him, that Phillips, who was at Puttealee, only eight miles off, had been joined by Bramley, with a large body of horse, and that they would at once commence restoring order in the district. This was most cheering news [for me. I sent off a messenger at once

how soon multitudes collect for this lawless purpose, and how completely they do their work, almost rooting up, as it were, the place attacked.

to Phillipps, informing him of the Budaon disaster, and saying we would join him in the evening. About 5 P. M. a reply was brought, and disheartening enough it was; saying that Bramley had only brought a few horsemen with him, and recommending me to join them immediately, as it was their intention to make at once for Agra. We thought it as well not to communicate this news to our host, and we left him immediately; reaching Puttealee about 7.

I found Bramley and Phillipps in very low spirits; and no wonder, for they informed me that news had just reached them that the body of horse which had been sent to their aid, consisting of Oude Locals from Lucknow, had the day before murdered their officers on the line of march, and proceeded in a body to Delhi; and that the guard with themselves, composed of sixty men from their homes on leave from different regiments, were not to be depended on, but were supposed to be in league with the Oude mutineers, and might rise and murder us at any moment.

We remained the 3rd and 4th at Puttealee with these fellows all round us, and very anxious. On the 5th, we got rid of the greater number of the troopers, by sending them nominally to guard a Tehseeldaree, some twenty miles off, in which there was a considerable sum of Government money. We heard afterwards, that immediately on reaching the place, these fellows seized the money, and then went off; some to their homes, some to join the mutineers.

A fine old Resseldar of Liptrot's Horse remained with us, and about twenty troopers, upon whose fidelity he said we could depend. I had frequent communications with this old officer (who, by the way, is now, I hear, in high favour with the Nawab of Futtehghur, and commanding some of his troops,) as to the causes of disaffection in the native army. He never mentioned the cartridges, or fear of outrages on their religion, as the causes, but ascribed them to the great dissatisfaction which existed at the acts of the Government, in the curtailment of furloughs and other privileges, the levy *en route* to their homes, from sepoys, of tolls at Ghauts, and in Government Seraiees, from which payments they were formerly exempt, being treated as a privileged class; also the distance they had to serve from their homes.

On the afternoon of the 5th, an anonymous note

was brought to Phillipps, stating that 200 mutinous sepoys were at a place some ten miles off, who intended coming to attack Puttealee the next morning, as they heard the district officers were assembled there, and had much treasure with them. This intelligence determined us at once to start for Agra, and preparations were made for leaving as soon as the moon rose, at 10 P.M.

I received, about the same time, a communication purporting to be from some of my friends in Budaon, stating that the mutineers had decamped from thence with the treasure, after firing the place and destroying all the buildings, and had gone back to Bareilly, and urging me strongly to return, as there was no longer any danger. I despatched a reply, saying that I was quite willing to do so, provided they would send me a sufficient force for my protection to the bank of the Ganges to conduct me to Budaon; and stating that I would remain at Puttealee till I heard it had arrived. I sent by the messenger also a note to my wife at Nainee Tal, telling her what had occurred, and that I was safe thus far.

Phillipps and Bramley, however, both urged me so strongly not to return to Budaon, but to accompany them, that I acceded to their representations, and gave up my intention. We set off; the sowars with the old ressaldars led, a number of half-armed thakoors followed next, and we ourselves brought up the rear. We feared that the sowars might prove treacherous on the way and attack us, so the thakoors were interposed between us and them, in order that if they *did* charge down upon us they must first pass through that body, and we should thus have warning of their intentions. We marched about four miles, when we thought that what we feared had actually occurred, and that we were at once to be attacked, for there was a sudden halt and a great noise and rushing about in the front. It was caused by one of the sowar's horses, a mad, vicious brute, which, having thrown his rider, came charging down upon us, and galloped back and forwards through the body of foot and horse, until he was stopped by a severe spear wound administered by a sowar whose horse he was attacking.

We marched without any other interruption all night, only halting once or twice to rest the men and horses. As the morning dawned we found ourselves in the neighbourhood of a small fort, about five miles from the Grand Trunk Road. Those inside threatened to fire upon us unless we halted and told who we were. The killahdar was one of our own zemindars; and after a parley with Bramley, with whom fortunately he was previously acquainted, he allowed us to enter the place and rest, while we sent out for information as to the road being clear in our front towards Mynpoory, for which place we were marching.

The messenger despatched for this purpose soon returned with the very alarming intelligence that there was a body of mutineers, horse and foot, on their way to Delhi, halting in our immediate vicinity, and completely blocking up the road in our front. We immediately consulted together on what course to pursue; the zemindar insisting on our immediately removing from his fort, which he feared would be attacked by the mutineers, as soon as they heard of our being in it.

We at first thought of making an attempt to cross the road in front of this body, trusting to the speed of our horses to escape, if we were pursued. On consultation, however, this plan appeared too hazardous, and we determined to retrace our steps and remain in some village in the rear, until night fell; when we might hope to elude these troops, and escape past them to Agra through

Mynpoory. As we approached the village where we thus intended remaining, we thought it best to send on a sowar to see if the place was clear; we ourselves halting in a small grove about a mile off, where we were hidden from observation. It was very fortunate that we took this precaution, for our messenger presently returned, telling us the village was occupied by 200 mutinous sepoys; the very party who we heard intended beating up our quarters at Puttealee, and who, changing their intention, had moved off in this direction.

This intelligence caused us entirely to alter our plans, and, striking through the jungles and by by-paths, to return to Puttealee. The sowars under the ressaldar had by this time become very insolent in their bearing: probably in consequence of our having already dismissed our thakoor guards of infantry, who were quite knocked up with the night march. It became very desirable, therefore, to get rid of these fellows; Bramley accordingly called up the old ressaldar and told him we no longer required his services, or those of his men, and that they might return to Furruckabad, whence they had come, or go anywhere else they liked. The attitude of these fellows became at this moment most threatening;

they seemed just wavering as to whether they would charge down upon and destroy us, or go off and leave us. They consulted together for a moment—one of breathless suspense to us—and then, to our great relief, suddenly turned about and rode off. We now went on, changing our direction as soon as we lost sight of the sowars, with the view of preventing their afterwards following our movements.

We marched from 6 o'clock in the morning until the afternoon, when, completely exhausted by the terrific heat and dust, we came upon a small hamlet. There an old soldier, a pensioner of our Government, who had served in Affghanistan, greatly commiserated our position, and in answer to our request for water brought us milk and chupatties, which were most acceptable in our fainting state. We rested here for an hour, and on going away I offered the old man a little money in return for his hospitality. He flatly refused to receive it, saying, with apparently real sorrow, "You are in far greater need than I am now, who have a home, whereas you are wanderers in the jungles; but if ever your raj is restored, remember me, and the little service I have been able to render you."

We promised to do so, and then left him. Still going through the jungle, we reached Puttealee, thoroughly tired out, at nightfall, having been in the saddle continuously since ten the previous night; more than twenty hours. Here Bramley and Phillipps determined to halt one day and rest their horses, and then make a fresh attempt to reach Agra.

At this time we were under the impression that our safety was best consulted by separating from each other, instead of keeping together; and as I could not abandon the persons who accompanied me, but felt at the same time I had no right to add to Bramley and Phillipps' risk by imposing ourselves upon them, I determined to leave the latter to go on to Agra by themselves, and with my party to endeavour to get back to Budaon, and if possible push my way through that district to the hills. The two Messrs. Donalds, Mr. Gibson, and myself, therefore started from Puttealee about 11 A.M. of the 7th June, to return to Kadir Gunge. Phillipps, as I was leaving him, said in so marked a manner, "I feel certain and confident that we shall meet again," that I felt quite cheered about him and myself.

We passed unmolested through multitudes of

men who were crossing the road, laden with the plunder of some large village they had attacked and sacked during the night. The men of all the villages through which we passed were collected in bodies at the entrance of each, and, while quite respectful, crowded round us, asked eagerly, "When will your raj return? When will your raj return?—in ten days or fifteen days? We are worn out and tired with this continual watching and being on the alert in case of being attacked, and we long for peace and quiet again."

We reached Kadir Gunge about four in the afternoon, and were civilly, but very coldly, received by the zemindar, our host of two days previous. Since then he had heard of the mutiny at Bareilly, and the conduct of the regiment coming up to Bramley's aid, and the intelligence had a marked effect on his demeanour. He, however, said he would secure a boat to take ourselves and our horses to the Budaon side of the river.

Shortly after we were seated, there was an alarm of an attack, and a general rush of all the retainers to the tower where the stand was to be made; after about an hour's anxious waiting, intelligence was brought that the body of men who had been threatening the attack had gone off to plunder some other place in the neighbourhood. They passed, in number several thousands, within half a mile of us.

As we were sitting inside the house, and just about to start to cross the river, a traveller from the Budaon side entered the court outside, and from which we could not be seen. He was asked the news, and gave a dismal account of the state of the roads along which he had passed; all the villages having been plundered, and many burnt. He then said that a large body of horse was the day before at Kukorah (the village we had slept in on the 1st of June, and the place we were then bound for,) searching for the Collector (myself), and that they were now in a village opposite Kadir Gunge. This news determined me to remain where I was until the next day, in order to get some information if possible from Budaon as to the state of the district, and whether I could pass through it with any chance of safety. I accordingly sent off a note to a person I considered staunch in the town, and requested him to write an immediate reply. This I hoped would have reached us by the next morning, but no messenger returned. Wearily the day passed on until evening, when our host, who had been much displeased at our remaining so long with him, and had scarcely given us any food, came to say that the boat was ready to convey us to the other side of the Ganges, and that we *must* start at once.

There was no help for it, so we mounted and rode off; but on reaching the Ganges we found that the boat provided for us was too small to contain any one of our horses, and that we therefore could not cross. We in vain endeavoured to got another; and, much depressed, were at last forced to betake ourselves again to the zemindar. He was very rude on our arrival, but was at length pacified. He strongly urged us to abandon all thoughts of crossing the river into Budaon and to go on to Furruckabad; which place was sixty miles off, the road pretty clear, and the station still safe. He told us the reason why he felt certain that no mutiny had occurred there as yet was, that several of his people were prisoners in the gaol at that place, and had it been broken open, they would surely have come back to their homes in this village ere that time.

We were perfectly helpless, and determined to follow his advice. Doing so, has brought me indeed to this place of misery; but had I crossed into Budaon what might not have been my fate?

Byjenath's messenger, Khan Singh, informed me that the letter written to Puttealee to induce me to return to Budaon, was a trick of the sepoys to get me into their hands. They had therefore sent the horsemen to the bank of the river, in expectation of my crossing, to await my arrival and destroy me on landing. They had been greatly exasperated against me, and determined to have my life, in consequence of finding only one lakh and a half in my treasury instead of seven, as they were led to expect; they knew that the deficiency was caused by my having refused to receive their money from the zemindars, as I knew it would, in all probability, fall into the hands of the mutineers.

The zemindar gave us two footmen for guides, who conducted us through several villages where we were unmolested. At length, about midnight, I saw the guide who was immediately in front of me stop suddenly and make a sign to us to halt. We accordingly did so, and coming close up to us he silently pointed out a large body of men, apparently between two and three hundred, lying in a hollow among a few trees, a little to our left. We thought they were all asleep, and that we could escape their notice, when all at once they rose up as one man and came towards us. It was no use attempting to fly, for we should then have lost our guides, as we were mounted and they were on foot; so we stood fast. I told the guide to go forward to meet them, and explain who we were, He was a sharp fellow, for I heard him immediately saying we were "Sahibs," going to meet and bring back some troops who were coming up from Furruckabad to restore order. The villagers seemed quite satisfied with this information, and let us pass. They were lying out about a mile from their village, as an advanced picquet, in expectation of an attack, by one of those "Pukars" I have already spoken of, with which they were threatened. They were much pleased to hear that there was a prospect of order being restored by troops, and it was not for us to undeceive them. After leaving them we passed through the village, which was full of men; but they never noticed or stopped us, as we had been allowed to pass through their picquets.

About 2 o'clock A.M., the guides left us, having put us in the straight road to Futtehghur, and we travelled on by ourselves. Just as the morning dawned, we were much surprised to see an encampment about a mile to the right of the road; apparently of a considerable body of men, from the number of tents, and their being disposed in regular lines. There were, however, no sentries, nor any signs of life, and we passed unchallenged. After travelling the entire night, with only one halt of ten minutes to water the horses, we arrived about 8 A. M. at a considerable Pathan village called Kaim Gunj, where there was a Government tehseeldaree.

We rode into the enclosure and summoned the tehseeldar, who appeared after a considerable delay; he was a frail old man, but, as we afterwards discovered, with a noble heart; for, under Providence, he was the chief instrument in saving our lives at this place. By the time he came a considerable crowd had assembled round us, and the tehseeldar seemed anxious to get us to leave the tehseeldaree and go with him to the residence of Nuwab 'Ahmed Yar Khan,' a native gentleman of influence and the chief proprietor in the place; who, he said, would be happy to receive us, and who could protect us, as his house was situated within a walled garden. We accordingly removed to this place, distant about a mile from the tehseeldaree, and were at once led into the garden, and told to remain there until the Nawab could himself receive us. We sat down under the shade of the trees; for the heat was by this time intense. Presently the Nawab's brother, attended by three followers, all armed with double barrelled guns, came to look at us. He was quite intoxicated with opium, and very insolent and excited in his manner. He questioned us as to who we were, and on my telling him that I was the Collector of Budaon, and that the others were indigo planters and a Customs patrol, he turned to me and said, "You I know, and will protect you, as you are a Government officer; as for these fellows I know nothing of them, and will have nothing to do with them." I thought it highly probable, that, infuriated as he was with drugs, he might shoot down my companions at once, and they themselves quite expected he would fire on them. Fortunately, however, at this juncture the Nawab himself appeared, and the brother was at once taken away.

The Nawab was kind and polite in his demeanour, but seemed most reluctant to allow us to enter his house. After much demur he admitted us on my representing that we were greatly fatigued, and suffering much from the heat of the sun, as the trees afforded us no sufficient shelter. I told him we had no wish to remain with him, but were most desirous to press on to Futtehghur, and hoped he would get us a boat to take ourselves and horses down the river to that place. He professed his readiness to help us, and sent off a messenger to the Nawab Doollah, a relation of his (living at a place about eight miles off near the Ganges, called Shumshabad), who we were assured would order a boat to be in readiness for us by the afternoon. We were then conducted to the top of the house, and some food given to us. My two servants were not allowed to accompany us, but remained with the horses in the court-yard below.

As we were eating our breakfast, a messenger came in and whispered something to the Nawab, who was sitting with us. The communication produced an immediate change in his demeanour; he rose, saying we must at once start for Shumshabad, where the Nawab Doollah would receive us, and that he would himself furnish us with an escort of five horsemen under the orders of one of his relatives, by name Mooltan Khan; a fine powerful Pathan between forty and fifty years of age, who was also sitting with us.

Before taking leave of him, the Nawab required me to give him a certificate that he had treated us well and given us an escort. This demand is almost invariably a prelude to treachery, as persons to whom such documents are granted always consider their possession must clear them from all blame whatever may happen to the granters. I was, of course, forced to give the certificate. As we rode out of the gateway, Mooltan Khan whispered to me, "It is as well for us to go across the fields, and avoid all villages:" and he at once struck off at a rapid gallop.

After riding for about four miles, we halted, to allow the riding camel on which Mr. Gibson and Wuzeer Singh were mounted, to come up; they, with Mr. Donald, senior, who was on horseback, having fallen considerably behind. On riding up Mr. Donald said to me, "I have heard something which will make your blood curdle. Wuzeer Singh informs me, he overheard the Nawab's people and our escort, before leaving Kaieem Gunge, say that we were all to be killed as soon as we embarked on board the boat." I rode up to Mr. Gibson's camel and questioned Wuzeer Singh, who assured me that he believed, from what he had heard, it was their deliberate intention to murder us all. Of course I was much shocked; but what could we do? I merely said, in reply to Mr. Donald, that we were helpless, and must now go on with our escort, showing no doubt of their fidelity, and trust in God to protect us. After halting about ten minutes, we again set off at a gallop, Mooltan Khan leading, and shortly after arrived at the Nawab Doollah's. There we were received with great civility by the Nawab's head man, a Hindoo, who was sitting transacting business in an open verandah, surrounded by a number of people.

Several messages immediately passed between the Nawab and this official, who at last went to speak to his master, in the interior of the house. I took the opportunity to send him my compliments, hoping that he was well, and would see and assist us in procuring a boat to take us to Futtehghur. The man soon returned, saying the Nawab would not see us (which I thought a very bad sign); but that we should have a boat as soon as it could be prepared. He then recommended my sending intimation of our coming to the kotwal of Futtehghur, and he wrote a purwannah, or order, for me to sign, and I pulled off my signet ring to seal it.

Some of the party asked to be allowed to look at the ring, which was handed round the circle, duly inspected, and civilly returned to me. It required a great effort to maintain a composed and cheerful demeanour all this time; but we contrived to do so, and to converse with those present. After sitting about an hour, we were invited to adjourn to a bungalow of the Nawab's, built and furnished in the European style, to have some refreshment before starting in the boat. The Hindoo Kardar, Multan Khan, and our escort, accompanied us to this bungalow, and sat down with us. I ate, fortunately for me, some hard eggs, which sustained me well during the next eighteen hours.

I was about to lie down, and try to get some rest, for I was sorely fatigued, when my suspicions were aroused by Multan Khan coming up and saying, "I pity you from my heart." I asked him why? He was explaining that no boat had been prepared for us, and that we could never hope to reach Futtehghur alive, from the state of the villages and roads, when Mr. Donald, junior, who was standing at the window, called out to me in much alarm, that there was a crowd of armed men collecting round the house, and pouring into the compound. The Kardar almost at the same moment came up to me saying, "You must all leave this place at once; you will be all killed if you remain any longer. Return whence you came, and stick to the sowars who accompanied you from Kaieem Gunj." Our horses were immediately ordered and we mounted. As I rode out of the enclosure, I looked round for my two servants, but the crowd was by this time so great that I could not see them. My second horse, ridden up to this time by my Affghan servant, was standing at the door, and we begged Mr. Gibson to mount him; but he being an indifferent horseman declined, and then got on his camel. Up to this time, the the crowd did not meddle with us, and opened a way for us to pass through.

Mr. Donald, junior, and I were riding in front, accompanied by Multan Khan, and had advanced about 200 yards from the house, when we observed a body of horsemen drawn up across the road, in a grove immediately in our front, and waiting for us. Multan Khan pulled up his horse, and bade us at once return to the house, as the only chance of saving our lives; for he said that neither himself nor any of his men would advance with us another yard. It was out of the question to attempt to get through this body by our four selves, and so we turned back to the house.

I was some way in front, and riding along by the wall of the enclosure in which the house was situated, and not far from the gate, when the mob opened fire upon us, with savage shouts and yells. How I escaped I know not, for the bullets were rapping into the wall all about me; but my horse becoming very restive under the fire, plunged so much that they could neither hit him nor myself. Turning round to see what was going on behind me, I saw Mr. Donald, senior, without his hat, trying to get out of the crowd, and a number of men rushing in upon Mr. Gibson and striking at him with swords and sticks.

I now noticed Multan Khan and our escort galloping off, leaving us to our fate. My only chance was to attempt to rejoin them; so I called out to Mr. Donald, senior, to follow me, and drawing my revolver, put my horse right at the crowd as hard as I could go. They opened for me right and left, and I passed close to poor Mr. Gibson: I shall never forget his look of agony, as he was ineffectually trying to defend himself from the ruffians who were swarming round him.

I could render him no aid, and was only enabled to save myself through the activity and strength of my horse. Once or twice I was on the point of shooting some of the fellows, but refrained; thinking that threatening them with my pistol was more likely to deter them, as when once a barrel was discharged they might close in upon me, fancying that I could no longer hurt them.

I soon got clear of the mob, and joined Multan Khan and the escort, who had by this time halted. Mr. Donald, senior, followed me almost immediately: his horse was severely wounded by a matchlock ball in the near hind leg; but he was himself untouched. His son also rode up soon after; he had escaped unwounded, by riding through the town, and jumping his horse over a ravine where the fellows could not follow him. A man also joined us mounted on my second horse, a difficult animal to manage; he threw his rider almost immediately, then bolted, and was, as I imagined, lost.

Multan Khan and the others seemed by no means pleased that we had escaped, and were very threatening in their demeanour. I rode up to the former, and putting my hand on his shoulder, said to him—"Have you a family and little children?" He answered by a nod. "And are they not dependent on you for their bread?" I asked. He replied "Yes." "Well," I said, "so have I, and I am confident you are not the man to take my life and destroy their means of support." He looked at me for a moment, and then said, "I will save your life if I can: follow me." He immediately turned and set off at a gallop, and we followed him.

One of the sowars, a scoundrel belonging to the Mehidpore Contingent, and mounted on a poor horse, rode alongside of me, and said, "Give me your horse; mine is good enough for you." I put him off by some civil answer; but he was much enraged at my refusal, and remonstrated with Multan Khan for not at once murdering us. Finding he could not persuade him or the other sowars to attack us, he struck off to a village through which we were to pass, in order to raise the villagers to intercept and murder us. This caused Multan Khan to take a long circuit through the fields to avoid the village.

We reached Kaieem Gunj about 4 P.M., and were instantly told to ascend to the roof of the house and show ourselves to no one. We were almost immediately informed that poor Mr. Gibson, who had been with us a few hours before, had been cut in pieces by the mob. The Nawab visited us soon after our arrival, and seemed heartily sorry for what had occurred; attributing the attack made upon us, and very justly, to the treachery of the Nawab "Doolah" of Shumshabad. He then plainly told us, that he could afford us no protection; that the people believed that we were covered with rings and jewels, and that the very children would tear us in pieces, if they saw us, to plunder us. I told him that we had nothing with us. But he said the story that I had produced my signet ring to seal the purwannah at Shumshabad had got about, and they believed we were covered with jewels, and that nothing would persuade them to the contrary. He said he could only consent to keep us in his house until nightfall, when we must quit it. I told him I would try and return by the way I had come, to my own district, where I thought friends would protect me. The Nawab said this was impossible, as I should be cut to pieces within the first mile.

I then said that we would try and make for Futtehghur. The Nawab allowed this was our best plan, but he at the same time declared his inability to get a guide to conduct us; alleging as the reason, that news had been received of the total destruction of our army before Delhi, and the death of the Commander-in-Chief; who had poisoned himself, though we gave out he had died of cholera. I represented that without a guide we must perish by the way; but he was immoveable, saying he could not help us, for no one would consent to aid or conduct us. Mr. Donald, senior's, horse was reported quite unable to move, from his wound, and it became necessary to supply his place. After much trouble, the Nawab procured for him in the Bazaar, for fifty rupees, a miserable pony, quite unsuitable for so heavy a man to travel with at any pace.

After the Nawab left us, we all three joined in prayer, thanking God for our preservation in the midst of such great danger, and entreating Him mercifully to open a door of escape for us, or if not to prepare us for Himself. I then sent for the old tehseeldar, who had befriended us in the morning, and on his coming pointed out to him the hopelessness of our ever reaching Futtehghur if we had to keep to the main road and pass through the villages, and that therefore we must have a guide to lead us through by-paths and fields. I begged him earnestly to go to the Nawab and try and induce him to give us at least one horseman as a guide. He consented to go, but expressed himself very hopeless of a favourable result; saying, if he succeeded he would come back again, but if he failed he would not return, as it would be only painful for him to part from us again. I then took off my watch and ring, as I had little or no hope of surviving, and made them over to him, to give to the first European officer he might meet, for conveyance to my family; he then left me.

My two poor companions had been fast asleep during this conference, and I now lay down myself, and fell into a light slumber, in which I continued for about an hour; when I was awoke by the voice of the Nawab saying, "He is asleep; don't let us rouse him: he is in need of rest." With inexpressible delight, I then heard the old lame tehseeldar shuffling up and saying, "it is never too soon to waken up a man if you have good news for him." I started up and called them both in, when the Nawab told me he had prevailed on two trusty men, connections of his own, to convey us safely to Futtehghur, and that we must start in two hours thereafter. He also gave me the satisfactory intelligence that my second horse had been recovered, and was in the stable and of course available for Mr. Donald, senior.

He and the tehseeldar then left me, enjoining me to lie down and sleep, and promising to come back soon, with native clothes in which to disguise us. They returned at the appointed time, accompanied by our friend Multan Khan. I then roused up my companions, and we were dressed in the Nawab's clothes; every article of our own dress, down to our boots, being burnt in our presence, to destroy all traces of us in the house. I only contrived to save my Testament and my darling May's purse; from which, however, I had to cut off the silver rings and tassels, lest they should attract notice. I put these, with my ring and watch which the old tehseeldar returned to me, in my waist-belt. The Testament I have still with me, and it has been my solace in many an hour of anguish and peril; but alas, the purse I dropped on the road and never saw again. I weep now when I think of that loss, and am not ashamed to say so; for sorrow and anxiety such as ours make the heart very ready to overflow at any remembrance of those we love, and whom it is probable we may never again meet in this life.

When all were ready, and our turbans, the

most difficult part of our costume to arrange, put on, we descended to the courtyard and there found our horses and the two guides ready. I mounted, but found to my dismay that my own saddle (an excellent Wilkinson and Kidd) had been removed, and replaced by a miserable article without any stuffing, which I feared might seriously injure my horse's back and render him unserviceable. A glance at one of the guides, a fine tall man mounted on a good looking bay mare, showed me that he had appropriated it; but it was no time for remark, far less remonstrance. The Nawab dismissed us very kindly, saying to me, "You make a very good Pathan in this dress; but mind, never venture to speak, or you will be at once discovered; the other two may speak, for they are country born, and have the native accent."

We rode slowly, and in profound silence, through the town of Kaieem Gunj, in which no one was stirring. Immediately on getting beyond it, the guide on the bay mare set off at a gallop, and led us through fields and through by-lanes for several miles without a halt. We had not proceeded very far when my little horse, who notwithstanding my having scarcely been off his back for the past week, was pulling hard, ran me under the branch of a tree, and knocked off the turban which had been arranged with so much care. I was hopeless of being able to put it on again, as none but a native can do this, and that only after the education of years; but happily I caught one end of it as it fell to the ground, and, tying a knot in my curb rein and taking it in my teeth, managed to guide my horse, while I contrived to replace my turban; though not in a way to escape detection, had we been stopped and examined.

After going about eight miles we halted to breathe our horses, and I took the opportunity of having some talk with our guide. He turned out to be a trooper of Cox's troop of Horse Artillery, on leave at his home in Kaieem Gunj. He assured me that 6,000 rupees would not have induced him to guide us, or give us any aid, had it not been for the earnest solicitations of his near relation the Nawab, to which he at last yielded. He was a splendid horseman, and had many a fight with the mare, a most vicious brute; which I watched with intense and breathless interest, as on the result my safety mainly depended. For the first few miles she went on without a check, but afterwards, and when it was highly important for us to go at speed, the brute would suddenly stop, rear and plunge, and do everything to get rid of her rider; but it was of no use. He stuck to the saddle as if he was glued to it, and at last he would force her on.

After riding about two hours, we approached two villages close to each other, and between which we had to pass. The one on the right was in flames, and surrounded by a band of marauders, who were busily engaged in plundering it. As we came on at full speed, the fellows caught sight of us, when within about a mile of the village. They raised a tremendous shout, and commenced rushing to a point where they hoped to be able to cut us off. *Then* we did ride for our lives; our guide leading us with admirable decision and sagacity. It was a most exciting race for about fifteen minutes. The shouts and yells of these miscreants, and the noise of the flaming villages, excited our horses to such a degree that they needed no urging to do their best? Both mine behaved nobly: Jan Baz, carrying his fourteen stone rider as if he was a feather, and my own little Cabulee tearing along and clearing every obstacle as if he enjoyed the fun.

The excitement was so great, that I quite forgot

the danger for the moment; although for some time it was doubtful whether we could clear the mob or not: we just succeeded in doing so, with about two hundred yards to spare; and I shall never forget the yell of rage the fellows raised when they saw they had missed their prey. Happily they had no firearms, and we were therefore quite safe from them, after we had once got beyond them. Had Donald been mounted on the miserable pony he purchased, instead of my horse, we must all have perished; as he never could have gone the pace, and we of course could not have deserted him: we must all have been cut to pieces. The recovery of my horse, and his being available for Donald to mount, when I thought him lost for ever, was but one of the many instances of God's merciful interference on our behalf to preserve our lives which I have thankfully to acknowledge.

About 4 A.M., as morning dawned, we neared Furrukabad, having ridden about twenty-four miles. Our guide pulled up at a Faqueer's hut for a drink of water, asking at the same time the news. In the grey morning light the Faqueer did not recognise us as Europeans, and told our conductor that all was as yet quiet in Furrukabad, the regiment still standing; that the station had been deserted by the Europeans, but the Collector Schiby Probyn was still at his post; and that the previous day a portion of the regiment had put down a serious mutiny in the gaol, killing many prisoners who were trying to make their escape. We were much comforted by this intelligence, and rode on with our guard to the public serai, in the town, where we dismounted without attracting any notice, and walked our own horses about, native fashion, to cool them. Our guide then left us, and went to the kotwallee for news, but soon returned, bringing a chuprassee with him to conduct us to the Collector's house. We remounted, our guides continuing with us for a short way: suddenly they left us, and I have never seen or heard of them since. Right well did they do their duty to us; and I will do my best to requite them, if my life is spared through these troubles.

We reach Probyn's house about 8 A.M., and as we entered, and received his hearty welcome, none of us could speak, from emotion; it took us some minutes ere we could explain to him where we had come, and what had occurred to us by the way.

Probyn then gave us an account of matters

at Futtehghur and elsewhere in his neighbourhood; which was far from cheering. He informed us that the 10th Regiment N. I., which formed the Futtehghur garrison, had already broken out into open mutiny, and threatened its officers, but had been temporarily brought back to its duty, and was than apparently staunch; though in his opinion not to be depended on. The European residents, with the exception of the officers of the 10th Regiment and Major Robertson, in charge of the gun carriages manufactory, had, in consequence of the state of the regiment, left Futtehghur; some of them had proceeded in boats to Cawnpore, and others, including Probyn's wife and children, were at a fort across the Ganges, in Oude, belonging to a zemindar of considerable influence named Hurdeo Buksh, who had offered to protect them.

Probyn urged us very strongly to join this party: we were, however, most desirous of proceeding down to Cawnpore by boat; and this plan we should no doubt have followed, but (most providentially for us) intelligence, which appeared to be authentic, reached Probyn during the day that the troops there had mutinied, burned the cantonments, and attacked the Europeans.

We then wished to make for Agra; but Probyn declared this impracticable, from the state of the roads and the large bodies of mutineers passing up towards Delhi. There was nothing for it, therefore, but to follow Probyn's advice; and happily, for me at least, it was that I did so.

We remained this day, the 9th of June, at Futtehghur. While there, Colonel Smith, commanding the 10th N. I., and Major Vibart, of the 2nd Light Cavalry, called upon me; the latter, when on his way to join his own regiment at Cawnpore, had volunteered to remain with Colonel Smith, who gladly availed himself of the offer. Major Vibart had commanded the party of the 10th N. I. who the day before quelled the riot in the gaol; and he had received on that occasion a severe contusion under the left eye, from a brickbat thrown by one of the prisoners. Both he and Smith seemed very sanguine that the regiment would remain faithful; more especially as news had just been received of a successful action against the mutineers near Delhi, by the Meerut troops under General Wilson.

We remained at Futtehghur until the afternoon of the 10th, when we crossed the Ganges and joined the party at Dhurumpore. Hurdeo

Buksh's fort. The heat was most intense; the sun blistering my hands into a mass of pulp, but doing me no further harm. We found a large assemblage of people congregated in the fort; among them the Judge of Futtehghur, Thornhill, the Rev. Mr. Fisher, and my former assistant at Budaon, Robert Louis, with their wives and children. This party had been already some days at Dhurumpore, and were very much dissatisfied with their position. I must say I thought very justly; for the fort was in so dilapidated a condition that successfully to defend it against any organized attack of the mutineers was quite hopeless. The accounts they had heard of the 10th N. I. putting down the outbreak at the gaol and returning to their duty, led them to believe that there was no longer any danger to be apprehended from that regiment, which would now continue staunch. They accordingly determined to abandon Dhurumpore, and return in a body to Futtehghur, notwithstanding Probyn's repeated remonstrances against the step, and his assurances, from the information he possessed, that the regiment was not to be depended on, and only remained true to its duty until such time as they found it convenient to mutiny; which depended on the movements of other mutinous corps with whom they were in daily correspondence.

Probyn himself, and his family, consisting of his wife and four children, determined to remain under Hurdeo Buksh's protection; an act which the party leaving considered one of great and foolhardy rashness. I at first intended to accompany them back to Futtehghur, along with the two Donalds, who were also returning; when a sudden thought struck me that I had better stay with Probyn, and I asked Hurdeo Buksh's agent if his master had any objection to my doing so. He at once, on behalf of his master, begged that I would remain. The party left Dhurumpore the night of the 11th and reached Futtehghur next morning.

On the 12th I received letters from Lowis and Vibart begging us to join them, assuring us that the regiment was quite staunch, and that we were in much danger at Dhurumpore, as Hurdeo Buksh would certainly fail us, if any pressure was put upon him. I showed these communications to Probyn, who expressed complete confidence in Hurdeo Buksh, and none whatever in the fidelity of the 10th. His prognostications proved correct; showing the accuracy of the information on which he had been acting throughout. Had Colonel Smith and the other officers of the 10th, as well as the others attached to the station, listened to his advice, the fort of Futtehghur would, early in May, have been provisioned and garrisoned by pensioners, and others to be depended on; and so all the calamities which subsequently occurred would, in all probability, have been averted. Providence, however, ordered it otherwise.

About 10 P.M. on the evening of the 13th, as I was lying half asleep, I was aroused by hearing a familiar and welcome voice saying, "Tell the Sahib, Wuzeer Singh has come;" I instantly jumped up and called him in, right glad to have him again with me. He informed me that on being separated from me in the crowd at Shumshabad, and seeing me ride off, he had no hope of rejoining me; he had, therefore, to ensure his own safety, concealed himself among the bushes in the garden. There he remained during the attack made upon us till the crowd dispersed, and was lucky enough to escape notice. He saw poor Mr. Gibson cut to pieces, and his body lying at the gateway, where it remained until the evening; crowds of the villagers coming up to look at it, yelling round it, and exhibiting the greatest demonstrations of joy at the sight—as he expressed it "rejoicing as they do at a marriage." At nightfall two sweepers dragged off the body and threw it on a dunghill, where it was devoured by the dogs. He also saw the poor man's riding camel taken in triumph into the inner court of the Nawab Doolah's house, to be exhibited to him. Wuzeer Singh lay close the whole of that night, and the next day, until evening; when he was discovered by a man, who, however, did not give information, but pitying him brought him a little food, and told him that I had not been killed, but had escaped into Futtehghur.

At nightfall Wuzeer Singh left his place of concealment, and, in consequence of this intelligence, made his way to Futtehghur during the night. Reaching it early in the morning he searched for me in vain through the cantonments. At last hearing that some Europeans were still at Dhurumpore, he made his way across the Ganges, in hopes of finding me among them; in which he was successful, as I have already described. He brought with him the whole of the money with which I had entrusted him on starting from Budaon; as also my gun, which he had contrived to carry off safe from the midst of the enemy.

For two days after the return of the Europeans to Futtehghur, all went well, and the 10th did their duty as usual.

Suddenly the 41st N. I., which had been quartered at Seetapore in Oude, having mutinied and massacred the Europeans there, and marched towards Futtehghur, were reported to have arrived on the bank of the Ganges opposite Furrukabad. On this intelligence reaching the 10th, it at once rose in mutiny. Fortunately, this occurred early in the morning of the 14th of June; and as the Europeans, who had taken the precaution since their return of sleeping in the fort, had not then left it, they escaped being massacred.

The first act of the regiment was to march to the Nawab, lay the colours of the regiment at his feet, offer him their services, and fire a salute in his honour. The first intimation we received of what was going on was the firing of this salute; which, as it consisted of 30 or 40 guns, fired very irregularly, native fashion, we imagined must be an attack on the fort. We saw at once, from the consternation excited thereby among Hurdeo

Buksh's people, that there was not much to be expected from them, should the mutineers make any attack upon Dhurumpore.

During the day we received very conflicting reports from Futtehghur: at one time, that the 41st were not going near the town, but straight on to Delhi, and that the 10th had sent them word that if they advanced nearer than the bridge, they would attack them. We were then told to keep quite close within a room, to avoid being seen, and to admit no one. While sitting there, we were disturbed by a knocking and digging at one of the outer walls of this room, which continued many hours. The noise suddenly ceased, and on going out one evening, as we were permitted to do, were much surprised to see that a fine 18-pounder gun had been dug out of the wall; where it had been concealed since the proclamation issued last year by the Resident at Lucknow to the Thalookdars of Oude requiring them to give up all their ordnance. A 24-pounder was at the same time produced from a field, where it had been concealed about fifty yards from a Neem tree, which marked its position. The wheels and other portions of the carriages of these guns were fished up from wells, where they had been hidden. Four other guns of different calibres were brought in from the chief villages in the neighbourhood, where they had been concealed; and all six were mounted and in position in the court-yard ready for service by night-fall. We heard that there were many more guns which could be produced if need be.

The guns were not brought into position sooner than they were required; for suddenly, about 8 P.M., there was a great commotion in the fort, and messengers despatched in fiery haste in different directions to collect the chief's feudal retainers; the alarm having been given that a large body of mutineers had crossed the Ganges, and were marching towards Dhurumpore to seize the two Collectors (as Probyn and myself were called), and plunder the fort. In an incredibly short space of time nearly one thousand people, all armed with some weapon or other, had, in answer to their Chief's summons, assembled at his residence, ready to do their best to oppose the expected enemy. The guns, with these retainers in the rear, were drawn up just outside the gate of the fort; and there Probyn and I joined Hurdeo Buksh. We were far from being favourably regarded by his people, who looked upon us as the proximate cause of the mutineers advancing on Dhurumpore: the latter having been attracted by the report, quite false though very generally believed, that Probyn had removed to Hurdeo Buksh's care several lakhs of the Government treasure; which they, of course, wished to appropriate.

Scarcely had we joined Hurdeo Buksh, when he intimated to us that we must at once leave Dhurumpore, and proceed to a small village across the Ramgunga, three miles off, where some connections of his own would receive and conceal us. This move he declared would not only ensure our safety, but his own also; as he said he should then be able, if the mutineers did actually come to Dhurumpore, to show them the interior of the fort and convince them we were not within. Probyn and I demurred greatly to this plan at first. Probyn said to me, "It is better to die fighting where we are, for if we once leave Dhurumpore we shall have our throats cut in half an hour." I saw, however, that Hurdeo Buksh was in earnest, and that he would on no account permit us to remain longer with him. I therefore went up to him, and seizing his right hand, said that we would at once go, if he would pledge his honour as a Rajpoot for our safety. This he at once did, and that most heartily, saying—"My blood first shall be shed before a hair of your heads are touched: after I am gone, of course, my power is at an end, I can help you no longer."

I knew of old that when a Rajpoot Chief once gave his right hand and pledged his honour, his word might be fully depended on; and I told Probyn and his wife that I thought we ought to lose no time in moving off and doing as Hurdeo Buksh desired us. We accordingly gathered together our bedding and a few things for the four children, and started: Mrs. Probyn carrying one child, I the baby, Wuzeer Singh a third as well as my gun, and Probyn's servant the fourth child. Probyn himself carried his three guns and ammunition. How thankful did I feel at that moment that my wife and child were, as I hoped, safe in the hills, and that I had to face alone these alarms and perils.

We had to walk for about a mile till we reached the ferry of the Ramgunga, where we were detained for a long time waiting for a boat. At last it came, and we crossed about midnight.

After walking about two miles on we reached the village of "Kussowrah," and were very civilly received by the Thakoors, who were uncles of Hurdeo Buksh; but of an inferior rank, as their mother had never been married to their father.

We were led through several enclosures to an inner one where there were cattle penned, a mare with her foal, and several goats. This, we were told, was to be assigned as our quarters: some of the animals were cleared out for us, the rest, we were promised, would be removed next morning. We found it impossible to sleep from the excitement, the filth of the place, and the effluvia of the animals, and were very miserable and depressed. In the morning we contrived to make ourselves more comfortable, our four-footed companions having been sent out to graze.

We were informed that a body of sepoys, two hundred and fifty strong, belonging to the 10th Native Infantry, had actually crossed the Ganges the night before, giving out that their intention was to attack and plunder Dhurumpore, and seize and murder us. This body advanced to within a short distance of the place, when they suddenly struck off towards Lucknow. They had with them three lahks of treasure, which they had contrived to remove from Futtehghur without the knowledge of their comrades, who were deceived by their story that they were only going to Dhurumpore and would rejoin them next day.

Hurdeo Buksh's people wished to attack and plunder this party; but he very wisely would not permit them, because, as he subsequently told us, he "feared that if once his people got the taste of plunder, he would never after be able to restrain them." This party accordingly passed through his estate perfectly unmolested; but as soon as they crossed his border they were attacked by the villagers of the next Talooqua, plundered, and destroyed. They were accompanied by an officer of the 10th Native Infantry, whom they had promised to convey safely into Lucknow; and on being attacked by the villagers, they desired this officer to leave them, as they said it was on his account they were attacked. This he was forced to do; and after wandering about for some time, as we afterwards learned, he received a sun-stroke while crossing a stream, and was carried in a dying state into a village, where he shortly after expired.

We remained perfectly undisturbed at Kussowrah up to Sunday, the 20th of June; when we were startled, about 4 A.M., by hearing heavy guns open. At first we hoped it might be a salute, but soon recognised that peculiar sound of shotted guns, so different from that emitted by blank cartridges; which, as well as the rapid and continued fire, convinced us that it was an attack on the fort. We were able also to distinguish replying guns. The fire slackened for a short time during the heat of the day, but towards evening became very heavy; it continued so all night and next morning until midday, when it again slackened; but only to recommence, as on the previous day, with increased fury. There was one very heavy gun which was discharged every five or ten minutes during the whole time, and we always encouraged ourselves by imagining that this was one of those in the fort; which we earnestly trusted was on each discharge doing much execution among the enemy.

Our anxiety during these miserable hours was well nigh overwhelming; forced as we were to remain inactive, and unable to aid in any way our poor beleaguered countrymen and women.

Probyn, on the commencement of the firing, sent a message to Hurdeo Buksh (for we were prohibited from going to him, and he never came near us), entreating him to send a body of his men to assist our people, and assuring him that in the event of their attacking the mutineers they would be handsomely rewarded. Hurdeo Buksh, however, sent a reply that it was quite impossible for him to do so; as his people, although quite willing to peril their lives in our defence, and in repelling any attack on Dhurumpore, would not consent to cross the Ganges, or act against the mutineers.

In the meantime, we were receiving the most conflicting reports of what was going on at Futtehghur; one man would come in and say that the mutineers could make no impression on the fort, and had suffered so severely from our fire that they had determined to abandon the attempt to take the place, and proceed to Delhi: scarcely had he left, when another of the villagers would cast down our hopes by informing us that our people were very hardly pressed, and were quite worn out by continual fighting; that their feet and legs were so swollen with the fatigue of standing day and night at their posts, that they resembled those of elephants, while their eyes were starting from their sockets for want of sleep: then an eager messenger would come in from Hurdeo Buksh, to say that he had sure intelligence that our people were all safe, and that the 41st Regiment was so dispirited that they were to raise the siege and move off next morning: no sooner had he delivered his news than we were told that the Nana had offered the mutineers a lakh of rupees (10,000*l.*) if they would carry the place by storm, and massacre the inmates, and that they were preparing to escalade that night. Matters went on in this way until the 22nd, when we prevailed on one of Hurdeo Buksh's men to try and make his way into Futtehghur, and learn how matters really stood. He went away, promising to bring us back news by the following night.

As we were sitting together on the forenoon of the 22nd, listening to the firing (which by this time was incessant), and in the deepest anguish of mind, Probyn received a note from our poor friend Robert Thornhill, the Judge of Futtehghur. The messenger who conveyed it had left the fort the previous evening; having eluded the besiegers by dropping down from the wall into the Ganges and swimming across. The note was written in great haste, and under deep depression, almost despair; informing us that they had been assailed without intermission for the past forty-eight hours by the 41st Native Infantry, who had been reinforced by the Mhow Pathans—that the garrison was completely worn out, and must all perish, unless God befriended them, and sent them some speedy aid. He implored Probyn to induce Hurdeo Buksh to go to their assistance with all the men he could muster: guaranteeing him in that case the highest rewards and pensions to all his men who were wounded, and to the families of those who might be killed.

Probyn accordingly again communicated with Hurdeo Buksh, by a messenger; but with no better success. We could, therefore, only send a reply to that effect to our poor friends in the garrison; and it almost broke our hearts to have to do so. Probyn advised Thornhill to endeavour to get the assistance of a body of men in Furrukabad, called "Sadhs;" a fighting class of religionists, who were supposed to be very hostile to the Sepoys and would act against them.

In the same afternoon we were visited by two bankers from Furrukabad. When they appeared, I said to Probyn that I did not like their manner, and was sure they were after no good, and were spies. He, however, said he knew them to be well-wishers. They expressed the greatest pity for our miserable position, shut up in a cowhouse without comforts of any kind, and with our lives hanging by a thread; they assured us of their great anxiety to help us in any way we could point out; and gave us very cheering accounts of Futtehghur, saying that the mutineers as well as the Mhow men were much dispirited, and that there was no danger of the garrison falling into their hands. They then left us, saying they would send us daily intelligence from Furrukabad of what was going on.

All this night the fire from both sides was incessant, and some persons belonging to the village, who had been in the neighbourhood of the Ganges during the day, told us, on their return, that the musketry fire was also tremendous and the loss on both sides very heavy.

About noon on the 24th, our messenger returned. He had contrived to make his way into the fort, and had seen and spoken with some of those inside. Among them to Thornhill, and Robert Lowis. He had been, he asserted, seized by the sepoys, and obliged in self-defence to drop a note he was conveying to me from Lowis, and which accordingly we never saw.

He told us that the case of those within the fort was desperate; that, although fighting with the most undaunted resolution, human nature could not hold out much longer; the entire remaining garrison having to remain on the alert night and day, and never for an instant leave their posts. Their original number of thirty-two fighting men was then considerably reduced; Colonel Tucker, Mr. Jones, and an artillery sergeant having been shot dead at their posts, Mr. Phillimore of the 10th wounded, and R. Thornhill having accidentally shot himself in the right arm. The ladies, women, and children, were shut up in Major Robertson's house inside the fort, where they were pretty safe from cannon shot. One of them, the wife of the sergeant who was killed, had been shot dead; having first avenged her husband's death by killing many of the mutineers with a rifle from the bastion, where she had taken her stand until killed. He told us that Colonel Smith, who was an unerring marksman, was killing numbers of the enemy with a pea rifle from his post on the wall, which he never left; and that Vibart, as we might have supposed from his undaunted character, was the real commandant of the fort, and going about among the thickest of the fire, directing and encouraging all. Our messenger, however, plainly said it was all in vain: that the defence could not be much further prolonged, as the ammunition of the garrison was failing, and the enemy had commenced mining the place, and, by an explosion on the previous day, had considerably injured one of the bastions. The mutineers had twice attempted to storm the fort by the breach thus formed; but were on both occasions driven back with heavy loss. They were led the second time by one of the Mhow Pathans, Multan Khan: to whom I had been so greatly indebted a few days previous. when the attack was made on us at Shumshabad. This man was shot dead on the top of the breach.

We were greatly distressed by this account of the state of things in Futtehghur, and also considerably alarmed for our own safety; as the messenger informed us that the two bankers who had visited us the previous day, had, on recrossing the Ganges, gone straight to the Nawab and Subahdar commanding the 41st Native Infantry, and informed them that they had just "seen the Collectors of Futtehghur and Budaon, who were concealed in Thakoor Kussuree Singh's bukree (farm-yard), on the eastern side just adjoining the road, where a few armed men could easily seize and destroy them." The Nawab and Subahdar, on receiving this intelligence, had said they would take measures for seizing us, as soon as the fort was taken and the troops were at liberty.

Two other miserable nights and days passed over us; the cannonade continuing as heavy as on the previous ones. Suddenly, about five in the morning of (I think) the 29th June, it entirely ceased. We at once imagined that the besiegers had stormed successfully, and we could only look at each other in silent anguish; feeling assured that our poor friends and acquaintances, men, women, and children, were at that moment being butchered by a blood-thirsty and merciless enemy.

All remained perfectly still for more than two hours. Wuzeer Singh went out to try and gather some intelligence, but returned unsuccessful—the villagers being quite as ignorant as we were ourselves of what had taken place.

It is impossible to describe the state of mind we were in. Suddenly we were aroused from a kind of silent stupor, into which we had fallen, by the renewed quick and irregular firing of heavy guns; the sound coming from another quarter than hitherto, and further down the river than Futtehghur. We were listening attentively to every shot, pacing up and down the narrow space allotted to us, and not daring to exchange a word with each other, when a messenger came in from Hurdeo Buksh.

This man had been sent to the bank of the Ganges as soon as the firing ceased, in the early morning, to ascertain the cause, and having delivered the intelligence he had gathered to his master, had been sent on to tell us the news. Disastrous enough it was: during the night the Europeans had evacuated the fort and betaken themselves to three boats, which had been secured before the siege and anchored under the river in face of the fort, ready for embarkation, if required. They had, of course, hoped to be able to float down the stream unnoticed, and to be, before the morning broke, beyond the reach of the sepoys' fire. Much time, however, had been lost in getting the women and children into these boats, together with the baggage, ammunition, and stores; so that they had only got a short way down the river when day dawned, and they were observed. As soon as they saw they were perceived and the alarm given, the boats made for our side of the river, and were dropping down the stream, when the heaviest laden grounded about three miles below Futtehghur, and remained immoveably fixed, notwithstanding all the efforts of the male portion of those on board, who got into the stream, to lighten and shove her off. It then became necessary to abandon this boat, and to summon back the nearest; which was obliged to work up stream, in order to take the passengers on board.

It was while engaged in transferring the unhappy people from the one to the other, that the sepoys, having dragged four heavy guns along the river bank opposite the boats, had opened on them. This was the fire which was then going on; and, as we feared, with inevitable fatal effect to all.

The messenger had left as the firing was being continued, and while the second boat, having taken on board its passengers, was endeavouring to drop down the stream. The only consolation he gave us was, that the boats were out of grape range, and that the firing being high, many of the balls had passed over the fugitives and buried themselves in the sand on the bank of the river. We begged of him to go off for more tidings; which we awaited with anxiety far too deep and terrible to be described. Men were every now and then rushing in with vague reports. At one time the boats were said to have sunk; at another they were reported floating down the stream unharmed, and beyond the range of the sepoys' guns. This we hoped was true, as the firing had gradually slackened, and then ceased for several hours.

About four o'clock in the afternoon, however, we were again aroused by the firing of heavy guns, apparently from a good way down the river, which lasted for about an hour. We remained in a state of the most painful suspense; but only the most conflicting rumours reached us, until late at night, when a horseman despatched to the river by Hurdeo Buksh, returned with the awful intelligence that of the two boats which had succeeded in escaping from Futteh-ghur, one had grounded near the village of

Singerampore, and remained immoveable, notwithstanding every effort to float her; the sepoys, who had been watching her movements from the bank, had dragged down two guns opposite this boat and opened fire upon her. Two boats full of sepoys came also down the stream, and as soon as they were within range opened a heavy fire of musketry on the unfortunate party; and when they had approached close enough, commenced boarding under the cover of this fire.

There was no help left. Of those in the boat, the greater number jumped into the Ganges and escaped a worse fate by being either shot down or drowned; some were massacred on board, and three or four ladies were taken prisoners and conveyed on shore. The other boat, which was considerably in advance, although attacked at Singerampore had contrived to escape, and was reported to have got safely away. It is said to have contained the Lowises and Thornhills. May God grant that the rumours which now reach us of its having safely reached Allahabad may be true.

This intelligence was too terrible for us to believe; and yet it was impossible entirely to discredit it. We trusted that in the morning better news might reach us. In the meantime we passed a miserable night, anxious and dejected; alternately sitting down, and rising up and pacing to and fro the small space of the enclosure. Earnestly and repeatedly did we three join in prayer, that God, in his infinite mercy, would shield and protect his poor people, "who were called by his name," and save them out of the hands of the enemy, and conduct them to some haven of safety.

The next morning the tidings of the previous day were confirmed. Of those who were in the last boat, none had escaped, except three of the ladies—Mrs. Fitzgerald, Miss ——, and Mrs. Jones, with her little daughter of eight or nine years old—who had all been taken to Furrukabad and made over to the Nawab: also one man, described to us as a sergeant, who had come ashore, desperately wounded, close to one of Hurdeo Buksh's villages, and had been immediately sheltered and cared for by his orders. This person we afterwards discovered was Major Robertson. All was now silent: the work of slaughter was over, and no more firing was heard. We were therefore left to brood over our own position, which now became one of extreme peril.

The sepoys of the 41st, the "Dubyes" as they were called, were now disengaged; and the Nawab, acting on the information as to our place of hiding, which he had received from the bankers, was reported to be about sending over a detachment to seize us. He sent messengers across to Hurdeo Buksh, informing him that the English rule was at an end; that he had killed all belonging to that nation, who had been stationed in Futtehghur, and demanded from him an advance of a lakh of rupees (10,000*l.*), as his contribution towards the expenses of the new raj. The Nawab, however, intimated at the same time to Hurdeo Buksh, that he was prepared to waive this claim, provided he would send him in by the evening the two Collectors' heads—Probyn's and my own. The intelligence of this demand having been made was soon conveyed to us, and we were told that Hurdeo Buksh had thought it best to temporize. He had therefore replied to the Nawab that he would think about the matter, and send an answer afterwards. We felt pretty confident that Hurdeo Buksh would not give us up; but we thought it best to do what we could for our own safety, and to encourage him to oppose the Nawab. We therefore begged of him to pay us a visit, as we were prohibited from going to see him at Dhurumpore.

After several days' delay; during which we were tortured by frequent reports of detachments of troops from Futtehghur being in full march on Kussowrah to seize us (which they might easily have done, had they been at all enterprising), Hurdeo Buksh visited us late at night. He was evidently in much anxiety, about the safety of himself and his family, which was seriously compromised in consequence of his having harboured us. He told us, that besides the communication already alluded to, he had received sundry other messages from the Nawab and the two subahdars in command of the mutineers, threatening, if he did not give us up, to take very complete revenge upon himself and his people.

He gave us at the same time a very deplorable account of affairs around us; saying that Nana Sahib had assumed command of the mutineers at Cawnpore, where the English had been so completely destroyed that not a dog remained in the cantonment; that Agra was besieged; that our troops at Delhi had been beaten back, and were in a state of siege on the top of a hill near there; that the troops in Oude had also mutinied, and Lucknow was closely invested.

He, however, assured us that he would never give us up to the Nawab; but, with his people, do his best to oppose any force which might be sent against Dhurumpore, from Furrukabad, for the purpose of seizing us: at the same time he said he thought his wisest course was to temporize. He had therefore sent a confidential agent to the Nawab to say that "he was with him, but as he had always, until the annexation of Oude, been immediately under that Government, he did not like to act without previous communication with Lucknow; to which place he had sent a messenger, informing the new authorities there that he had two Collector sahibs with him, and asking what he should do with them. If they did not otherwise instruct him, he would then make us over to the Nawab; but it was quite imperative on him, before doing anything, to await the return of his messenger, who might be expected in ten or twelve days. The Nawab and the subahdars had, Hurdeo Buksh informed us, expressed themselves satisfied with this explanation.

In this way he hoped to gain time, until the rains, now close at hand, fell; when the Ramgunga and Ganges would rise in flood, and the whole country be inundated, so that Dhurumpore and Kussowrah would become islands surrounded with water for miles; he might then defy the sepoys, as it would be impossible for them to bring guns against him, and they would not dare to move without artillery.

It was nearly morning when Hurdeo Buksh left us, not much encouraged by his visit, and in a state of great doubt and perplexity. The tone of the people had, since the fall of Futtehghur, much changed towards us: they had become insolent, overbearing and threatening; clearly giving us to know that they wished us no good, and that it was only the fear of the "Konwur," as they termed Hurdeo Buksh, that prevented their getting rid of us. A day or two after this, we were visited by a connection of Hurdeo Buksh called the "Collector Sahib," accompanied by another relation, who we knew bore the bitterest animosity towards us. We felt that their coming boded us no good, and it was with much anxiety that we received them and awaited their communication. They told us that it was quite impossible for Hurdeo Buksh to protect us any longer: he had already risked enough for us: we must now therefore leave his protection and shift for ourselves. He had, they told us, sent them to tell us to prepare to start in a boat down the Ramgunga for Cawnpore: which place they asserted had not yet fallen, and which we might easily reach. We remonstrated against this arrangement, telling them it was quite contrary to Hurdeo Buksh's own sentiments so lately expressed to us by himself. They, however, would listen to no expostulations, and ordered us to be ready to start by next evening, by which time the boat would be prepared for us. The two old Thakoors of the village, who ever since our arrival had been uniformly kind and civil to us, as well as Seeta Ram, a poor Brahmin who had shown us much kindness and sympathy, depriving his own family of milk to give it to Probyn's children, entreated us not to proceed in the boat; assuring us that if we did so the villagers on the banks would murder us before we had gone five miles down the stream. We tried to communicate with Hurdeo Buksh; but our messengers were not permitted to cross the Ramgunga, which lay between us and Dhurumpore: we were therefore quite helpless, and could only do as we were ordered, and prepare ourselves to go to what we felt assured was certain death. So convinced were the natives that the expedition would be fatal to us, that Probyn's three servants, hitherto faithful, refused to accompany him.

I then determined not to take Wuzeer Singh with me, but to send him to Nynee Tal with a farewell note and my little Testament to my wife, to tell her what had become of me. I summoned him for this purpose, and told him that he must now leave me, as I was going on a journey which would, in all probability, be fatal to us; that I could not allow him to perish on my account, which he would do if he accompanied us, and that he must try and reach my wife and tell her all that had befallen me. He expressed the greatest reluctance to leave me, and only consented to do so at my earnest and repeated solicitations. We then joined in prayer together, as I surely thought for the last time on earth. I implored him never to desert his faith or revert to idolatry; but, whatever happened, to cling to the Saviour he had once acknowledged. He wept much, and we parted; but, as it happened, only for a short time. In little more than an hour he came back into my room, and, throwing down the little parcel on the bed, said he could not go: he entreated that I might allow him to accompany me, saying, almost in the words of Ruth to Naomi, "Where you go I will go, and where you die I will die also." So determined was he to share my fate, that I was forced to consent to his accompanying me.

We had got our little baggage ready, and were prepared to start, almost resigned to our fate, when God in His infinite mercy, and in answer to our prayers, interposed to prevent our going. When the messenger appeared, about 8 P.M., as we thought to summon us to start, he informed us that the boat was not quite ready, and that we could not move that night. Thus were we reprieved, for the time as it were, from certain destruction: for not one of us expected to see the morning light. After this, we were allowed to remain for a day or two unmolested.

The Ramgunga having in the meantime considerably risen, we were then informed that the voyage was in consequence quite safe, and that as the boat was ready we must be prepared to depart in the evening. Again did the Thakoors and Seeta Ram implore us to refuse to leave the village; we were, however, quite helpless, and could only obey.

About 8 o'clock in the evening, I forget the

precise date, we started from the village to embark; Wuzeer Singh and two of Probyn's servants, who had on this occasion volunteered to accompany him, carrying our little baggage, and what necessaries for the boat we could collect; Mr. and Mrs. Probyn each carrying a child, and I taking the baby, the only one of the children who would come to me. The old Thakoor Kussuree came with us to the end of the village, but declined going any further; saying, he could not be a party to conducting us to what he knew was intended for our destruction.

The road leading to the Ramgunga from the village, was one mass of mud and water; poor Mrs. Probyn was scarcely able to wade through it, and we could afford her but little assistance. We had proceeded about half a mile in the direction of the boat, when a breathless messenger met us from Dhurumpore, telling us to turn back at once, and proceed to a village beyond Kussowrah instead of to the boat; as the sepoys were in full march from Futtehghur to attack Dhurumpore, and that Hurdeo Buksh had gone out to meet them with his people. We returned back in accordance with these orders; every moment expecting to hear the firing commence.

We had gone about three miles in the direction of the village indicated, where we were overtaken by a second messenger from Dhurumpore, ordering us back to the boat; as the sepoys, who had advanced some way towards Dhurumpore, had retreated, and were reported to be re-crossing the Ganges. Accordingly we again retraced our steps, and stopped half an hour in Kussowrah to rest; as Mrs. Probyn, who had on this, as on every other occasion, shown the most patient fortitude, was very much exhausted, and her clothes saturated with wet and mud. We were not allowed to remain long, but were ordered off, as we thought finally, to embark in the boat. God, mercifully, however, ordered it otherwise.

When about half-way between Kussowrah and the river, we held a consultation together: it was determined, as a last resource, that Probyn should go on ahead of us, try to get across the river to Dhurumpore, and procure an interview with Hurdeo Buksh; as we thought that by so doing, he might prevail on him not to expose us to a cruel death by sending us down the river without a guard, and with boatmen who would certainly desert us. He started; and Mrs. Probyn, the children, Wuzeer Singh, and I followed, and after much fatigue reached the bank of the Ramgunga. We were dismayed at finding the stream, instead of being in flood as we expected, a mere thread; so that the villagers on either bank could, without much difficulty, reach the boat with their matchlocks as it passed down, and destroy us. No boat, however, was on the bank, which was one mass of thick mud. A log of wood furnished a seat for Mrs. Probyn, who was by this time much exhausted, and a cloth was spread for the children on the driest spot we could find, where they slept in their innocence as soundly and securely as if they had been in their beds.

In this position we remained for about an hour, and were expressing our surprise that Probyn, who had crossed the river at the ferry, was so long of rejoining us; when we were hailed by a man, who, we saw by the moonlight, was approaching us from some distance down the stream. He proved to be the connection of Hurdeo Buksh who had visited us with the "Collector" some days previously, and we argued no good from his appearance. On this occasion, however, he agreeably disappointed our forebodings; for he gave us the welcome order to go back to Kussowrah, and there await further instructions. We accordingly set out: I took one of the children (Leslie) on my back, and carried in my arms, my poor little friend the baby: now "poor" no longer: for he is "before the throne of God," who has called him to Himself. We met one of the Thakoors, who lent his arm to Mrs. Probyn: she being too much fatigued to proceed without his help. We reached our old quarters about 3 A.M., soaking wet, and thoroughly worn out; as we had been moving almost continuously from 6 P.M. In about an hour after our arrival, Probyn joined us. He had been fortunate enough to see Hurdeo Buksh, who was at first displeased at his unexpected appearance; but after Probyn had explained, was very gracious, and assured him that for the present he would abandon all intention of sending us down the river. We then joined in prayer and thanksgiving to God for His gracious interference in our behalf, in thus delivering us in so remarkable a manner from this imminent danger; entreating, at the same time, His guidance and protection for the future.

After this, several days passed without much incident; except that Wuzeer Singh on one occasion came in to report that, when strolling beyond the village, he had met several men whom he at once recognised as sepoys, almost naked, and in a very miserable plight. He had learnt from them that they were deserters from the mutineers at Delhi, and when going home with their plunder, had been attacked and stripped by the villagers near Mynpoorie. They told him things were not prospering with the mutineers at Delhi; that they had suffered most severely, and were heartily sick of it. This intelligence was for the time cheering; but we were soon depressed by the news, brought to us almost simultaneously from Dhurumpore, that the Nawab and Subahdars were becoming more urgent with Hurdeo Buksh to deliver us up, and had repeatedly forwarded purwannahs ordering him to destroy us and send in our heads. They had even gone so far as to send him a firman, purporting to be from the Emperor of Delhi, conveying the Imperial order for our destruction.

Hurdeo Buksh sent his brother-in-law, one of his most confidential people, to us to explain how hardly he was pushed, and how much difficulty he had in protecting us. He had therefore come to the conclusion that our safest plan was to start for Lucknow, and was accordingly making arrangements for our journey there, and for securing protection for us by the way, through certain influential talookdars, friends of his. Hurdeo Buksh was led to recommend our going to Lucknow in consequence of the intelligence he had lately received, that the attack on the Residency had been signally repulsed, and the mutineers withdrawn from the town; and, as the place was well provisioned, and contained plenty of ammunition, there was no fear of the garrison being unable to hold out: more especially as none of the Rajwarrahs, as the chief talookdars are called, had as yet joined in the rebellion; but on the contrary had stood quite aloof from the sepoys.

We expressed to the brother-in-law our willingness, and indeed eagerness, to proceed at once to Lucknow, as recommended by Hurdeo Buksh, We were ourselves much pleased at the prospect of quitting Kussowrah, and finding ourselves once more among friends and countrymen. It was accordingly arranged that we should start on a certain night, as soon as it was dark, for Lucknow, by Sandee, which we were to reach in four marches. Our horses, which we had not seen since the 9th of June, were on the night appointed, sent up from Dhurumpore after dark, for the conveyance of Probyn and myself, and a palanquin was prepared for Mrs. Probyn, and the children. To avoid observation as much as possible, Probyn dyed his face, neck, hands, and feet, a dark brown. This was considered unnecessary for me; exposure to the sun having already made me almost as dark as a native, so I escaped a very disagreeable process.

We were sitting all ready to move, and, for the first time in many weeks, were in something approaching to cheerful spirits, when rain came on; and to our bitter disappointment, we were told that we could not in consequence start that night. The next day we were informed we must not move until Hurdeo Buksh came to see us again, and that the time of his doing so, depended on the return of a messenger he had sent to make some arrangements for us on the road. We had to wait four nights in this manner; feeling much chagrined by the delay, and accusing Hurdeo Buksh of supineness. On the fifth night he came about midnight, and was more depressed than we had ever before seen him; he informed us that the lull at Lucknow had been only temporary; that the mutineers, having been reinforced, had again attacked the Residency, and that fighting was going on without intermission, day and night. He told us that just as we were going to start for Lucknow, on the night first fixed for our departure, a rumour had reached him of the renewal of hostilities. He had accordingly seized the pretext of the rain falling to prevent our starting, and had continued to detain us until he could ascertain the real state of affairs, by sending a messenger to the spot. This messenger had only now returned, and confirmed the previous intelligence; leaving little hope that the garrison could long hold out against the multitudes attacking it. Our plan of going to Lucknow, was thus frustrated. Had we started as at first intended, we must have fallen into the hands of the mutineers, and been massacred. Again, therefore, had we to praise God for having delivered us from the imminent danger into which we were blindly rushing.

Hurdeo Buksh then gave us the pleasing intelligence, that the younger Mr. Jones and Mr. Churcher, two of the Futtehghur party, had escaped out of the boat which had been boarded near Singerampore by the sepoys, and were then concealed in one of his villages. They had been kept so strictly hidden by the herdsmen among whom they were, that the fact had only a few days before come to his knowledge; and he had given orders that they should be provided with both food and clothing.

The most appalling news, he, however, informed us, had reached him from all quarters. There was no doubt whatever of the fall of Cawnpore, where every European had been destroyed. The party who had gone down the river by the first boats from Futtehghur, the American missionaries, the Monctons, Brierly, &c., had, he heard, been attacked and massacred near Bithoor. Agra was reported to have fallen, and the Europeans destroyed there, while attempting to make their way in boats down the Jumna. The Bombay army had revolted; and, to crown all, there were no signs of aid coming, nor troops arriving from any quarter. Under these circumstances, he thought our only chance of safety was to remove secretly from Kussowrah — where the Nawab and sepoys, from the information given them by the bankers, knew we were living under his protection, and where we were never safe from attack — and go into hiding in one of his villages, situated about 20 miles distant, in a very desolate part of the country, and immediately on the bank of the Ganges. In order to maintain secrecy as to our position, the Probyns should only take one servant with them, while Wuzeer Singh should go with me.

On this proposal being made, I felt confident that if once we left Kussowrah and the protection of the Thakoors to proceed to the village indicated, we should be left entirely to the mercy of some of Hurdeo Buksh's people; who were most anxious to get rid of us, and who would use the opportunity of having us in their hands, to put us on board a boat, and make us descend the river: which would be equivalent to certain death. There was not a moment to lose; for go we must, should no other mode of providing for us than going to this village be determined on, before Hurdeo Buksh left. I whispered to Wuzeer Singh, who was kneeling behind me, during the interview, "You hear what the Chief says: if we go to the village, we shall be all killed; go out to the Thakoor Kussuree, and tell him what has been proposed, and beg of him to make some better arrangement for us." In a few minutes he returned, and said, "It is all right: as soon as Hurdeo Buksh goes, Kussuree will meet him outside, and offer to be responsible for us, and to conceal us in one of his own villages."

Soon after, Hurdeo Buksh took his leave of us, to return to Dhurumpore. I gave a sign to Wuzeer Singh to follow, and bring us back intelligence of what passed between Hurdeo Buksh and Kussuree. He soon returned, looking very cheerful, and told us that all had been arranged as proposed, and that Hurdeo Buksh was himself coming back to tell us of the change of plan. In a few minutes he came in, accompanied by Kussuree, and told us that Kussuree, thought he could hide us effectually in the jungle, in a village nearer than that on the Ganges: we had better go wherever he arranged for us, and put ourselves entirely in his hands. This we at once gladly consented to do; and Hurdeo Buksh left us.

Next day Kussuree informed me that he was now entirely responsible for our safety, and he feared he had undertaken more than he could perform. I encouraged him, saying we felt quite confident, and easy in our minds, as long as he remained with us. He then told me that it would be necessary for him to go out into the jungle—which extended for many miles towards the north-east, commencing two miles beyond the village of Kussowrah—and select a place in which we might be safely hidden. He proposed that he and Wuzeer Singh should ride out in the afternoon, for this purpose, on my two horses; which had been kept at Kussowrah ever since the night we were to have started for Lucknow. Of course I readily agreed.

At 4 P.M. they started, and returned about 9 P.M. Wuzeer Singh told me that they had proceeded far into the jungle, which was very dense, to a small village where we were to be concealed, and where he was sure that no one could find us if they searched for a year.

Kussuree and the other Thakoor, Paorun, came early next morning to explain to me alone, the plans they had formed for our future concealment and safety. These were rather startling. First, they insisted that it was quite hopeless to expect that our movements could be kept secret, or our position concealed, so long as we were accompanied by four children. It was therefore quite imperative that the Probyns should leave these behind in the village; where every possible care would be taken of them. If, as was very probable, the enemy came to Kussowrah and instituted a search for us, they could contrive to hide the children; and, if they were discovered, it was not probable that the sepoys, finding we were gone, would injure them. If they did kill them, there was, of course, no help for it; but it was their opinion that the chances of safety for the children were far greater separated from their parents than remaining with them. For ourselves, it was arranged that we should be hidden in the jungles all day, moving about from place to place as occasion might require, and returning, if we could, at nightfall to the little hamlet, which had been prepared for us to sleep in.

The plan appeared to me most impracticable, and I pointed out, that considering the season of the year, the rains being close at hand, it was not likely that any of us, certainly not Mrs. Probyn, could stand the exposure and fatigue of wandering about all day in the jungle, as they proposed. I reminded them that they had always told us Kussowrah would be a secure asylum as soon as the rains commenced, as it then became an island from the swelling of the rivers; and this must soon occur. Why, then, not let us remain for the present quietly where we were, to take our chance.

This both Thakoors declared to be impossible, as Hurdeo Buksh would not consent to our remaining any longer in Kussowrah. Had the usual rains fallen we might, they said, have done so; but they had hitherto failed, and the place was then quite open to attack. They further told me that although the village was quite safe from attack during the early part of the rains—being entirely surrounded by water deep enough to prevent any one reaching the place except by swimming and wading alternately, but not sufficiently so for boats; yet, as soon as the rains reach their height, a "sota," or channel, is formed, connecting Kussowrah with the Ganges and Ramgunga, and navigable for boats, by which the sepoys might reach us easily from Futtehghur without our receiving any intimation of their intentions: starting any night at sunset they might be upon us before morning. I then expressed my conviction that the Probyns would never consent to abandon their children, although they might feel quite convinced that the Thakoors would do all in their power to protect and preserve their lives. They, in reply, assured me that it was quite impossible to save us all, if we remained together; while by separating from the children all might possibly be saved. If, however, the children did perish, their loss might be repaired: their parents might have a second family; but they could never get second lives if they once lost those they had.

Finding the Thakoors immoveable, I said I would go out and discuss the matter with the Probyns, and let them know the result. I then informed the Probyns of all that had passed. They of course declared their determination not to part with the children. But then came the reflection, might they not be destroying any little chance of safety which remained for them by determining to keep the children with themselves? Was it not better to make them over to the Thakoors, and to trust that, in the very probable event of themselves perishing, the children, if saved, would be given up to some of our own countrymen as soon as Futtehghur was recovered? The hearts of the poor parents were torn with anguish; not knowing what course to adopt. The ayah was then asked if, in the event of the children being left at Kussowrah, she would stay with them; which she flatly refused to do. Mrs. Probyn then thought that she might, perhaps, be allowed to remain with her children; but

Probyn said he would never consent to leave her behind.

At last it was determined we should all remain together, and trust to the Almighty care, which had hitherto so graciously watched over us, to protect us still. We called in the Thakoors, and told them of our determination. They pitied us, and did not any longer insist on our immediately leaving Kussowrah; but said we might remain there for the present, as there was a good prospect of the rains falling soon.

Eagerly did we wait for their coming, watching with the most intense anxiety each cloud as it rose; and many a day of fair promise of torrents did we sadly see pass away without a shower. When there were no clouds in the burning sky over our heads, we tried to gather hope from the flight of the swallows; which the natives told us was a sure indication of rain when they flew near the earth. But day after day the rains held off; and there seemed a prospect of their even failing altogether.

The continued drought caused the hearts of the Thakoors to fail, and at last they fairly told us, they dare not keep us any longer in Kussowrah, but that we must start for a village in the jungle somewhere to the north; in which, they said, they had arranged to conceal us. That very day, they said, had been fixed on by the village astrologer as a lucky one for our start, and we were to move as soon as the moon rose at night. We all packed up ready for departure, and had gone in the meantime to sleep, when I was woke up by the Thakeer Paorun about 11 P.M., saying they had only just found out that the moon did not rise until three in the morning of the next day to that fixed on as lucky, and of which there was only one watch then remaining.

As we could not ourselves leave until the moon gave us sufficient light, it was imperative, he said, that something belonging to us should be sent on in the direction we were going—which the astrologer declared would as certainly secure the happy influence of the day as proceeding ourselves in person. A table-fork, the first thing that came to hand, was at once made over to Paorun, with which he went off quite satisfied; he sent it on by a bearer a mile on our proposed route, where it was, with due form, buried.

At 3 A.M., the Thakoors woke us up, and we started. An elephant had been procured for Mrs. Probyn, her ayah, and the children. Probyn and one servant (the other had absconded the night before), and I and Wuzeer Singh walked. When we were starting, I missed old Kussuree, and as I had great confidence in him, and remembered his own repeated advice—never to go anywhere if he did not accompany us, I waited for him; he, at last, and after sending many messages, joined us, but evidently with much reluctance. No sooner had we started than the rain came down in torrents, wetting us through, as also our little bedding. About a mile in advance of Kussowrah, we came on a stream of water so deep that the elephant could not wade across and was therefore dismissed. We had to be ferried over in a little boat, and then to proceed on our feet, each of us carrying a child, The path lay over ground thick with thorny bushes, which made our progress slow and painful. About a mile and a half from the stream we came to a large piece of water, which we had to wade across. Probyn carried his wife over, but with much difficulty, as it was deep and the bottom full of thick slippery mud.

At last, just as the day was dawning, the rain all the while pouring in torrents, we reached our destination; a wretched, solitary hamlet of four or five houses in the middle of the waste, and inhabited by only a few herdsmen and their cattle. The scene was desolate beyond description. As we came up, no one was moving in the village, all being yet asleep. One of the Thakoors roused up the chief man, a wild-looking Aheer, who pointed out to us a wretched hovel, which he said was for the Probyns. It was full of cattle, and very filthy: the mud and dirt were over our ankles, and the effluvia stifling.

My heart sank within me, as I looked round on this desolate, hopeless scene. I laid down the poor baby on a charpoy in a little hut, the door of which was open, and on which a child of one of the herdsmen was fast asleep. Poor Mrs. Probyn, for the first time since our troubles commenced, fairly broke down, and wept at the miserable prospect for her children and herself. Probyn was much roused, and remonstrated with the Thakoors saying, "If there is no better place for us than this, you had better kill us at once, for the children cannot live here more than a few hours: they must perish." In the meantime I had looked round, to see if any arrangement could possibly be made for sheltering them, and, observing a little place on the roof of one of the huts, pointed it out to Wuzeer Singh: he immediately scrambled up, and having examined it, called out that it was empty, clean, and dry, and a palace compared with the place below. I mounted up with his assistance, and was overjoyed to find a little room, clean and sweet, and with apparently a water-tight roof.

I called out to the Probyns below, and Wuzeer and I helped up Mrs. Probyn, and then the children; Probyn followed, and we, eight persons in all, established ourselves in this little space, most thankful to have it to shelter us, small as it was. The Thakoors made no objection to our appropriating the room, provided we kept strictly within it and never showed ourselves outside; as they feared we might be seen from the roof, and our hiding place discovered. We could only be contained in this room by lying down on the mud floor, in places fixed for each. One little corner was assigned to me, neither so broad nor so long as the smallest berth in a ship's cabin; where I deposited my blanket and the little bundle which served me as a pillow and contained all my worldly goods: merely a single change of native clothing, but quite sufficient; and really I don't know that any one, in the best of circumstances, requires more. Soon after we got into this place, the Thakoors took leave, promising often to visit us; they made over the charge of us to the Aheers, enjoining them to let no strangers enter or stop in the village on any account, and to maintain perfect secrecy respecting us. All which they professed their readiness to do; asserting that they would die for us rather than betray us.

The rain, which had come down heavily all the morning, now ceased, and for several days there were only occasional showers. The heat was intense, as we were so closely packed together in this little room. We could only get out at night; and during the day, the only relief we had was to turn on our backs, or from one side to the other, or sit up: standing or moving about was quite impossible. The poor children were in sad misery; they could not be allowed to leave the room and there was no space in it for them to crawl or move about. They were much more patient than we could have expected, and happily slept much. We were also now a good deal pressed for food; all we could get being a little milk and chupatties: and not the former on Sundays, as the Aheers will on no account part with the milk of their cattle on that day, but appropriate it for themselves. Notwithstanding our miserable circumstances, we lived with much harmony and in comparative peace. Thanks be to the Almighty! whose blessing and protection we duly implored together morning and evening; finding Him, as He will be found by all who seek Him, "a very present help in time of trouble."

Suddenly the rains came down with tremendous force, and neither Probyn nor I could sleep, as we had hitherto done, on the roof of the house just outside the door of our room, emerging therefrom at nights, when it fell dark. The space inside had become much circumscribed in consequence of leakage, one or two places in it having become untenable; I was, therefore, forced to try and secure some shelter for myself elsewhere. Wuzeer Singh succeeded in renting a cow-house for me for two rupees (4*s.*) a month: a small, miserable hovel in which two cows had hitherto been stalled. It was, as usual, without any door, and having probably not been cleaned out for years, was filthy beyond description. I was, however, thankful for this shelter, and Wuzeer Singh having cleaned it out, and contrived to hire a charpoy (native bed) for me, I was, as the roof did not leak, made comparatively comfortable. Many an hour of intense agony of mind, when I thought of all those dear to me, whom I was probably never to see again, and some also of blessed peace, have I spent in that little room.

The men of the hamlet used to come and visit and talk with me now and then. I had no means of keeping them out, even if I desired it, so they went and came just as they pleased. One day a relative of the chief man of the village, and residing at another not far off, arrived on a visit, and, of course, came to my room to have a look at me. He sat down, and we entered into conversation. I was surprised to find him much more quick and intelligent than the generality of the villagers, who were rude in the extreme; and found on inquiring that he had been a traveller, and had been, with his four bullock cart, attached to our commissariat during the first Sutlege campaign, when he went as far as Lahore. I inquired if he had been regularly paid for the duty: he assured me fully and liberally, and commenced praising the justness and liberality of our Government; under which, as he expressed it, "the lamb and the lion could drink at the same stream." It immediately struck me that I could perhaps induce this man to convey a letter to my wife at Nynee Tal; of whom on that date, the 17th July, I had heard nothing later than of the 26th May, and concerning whose safety and that of my child, I was in constant and terrible suspense: for could I be sure that Nynee Tal had not fallen as well as Bareilly and Futtehghur, and the dwellers there, as at the other places, fearfully massacred?

I told the man (whose name was Rohna) the misery I was enduring about the "Mem Sahib" and the "Baba;" that if I knew they were safe I could bear anything; and entreated him to take pity upon me, and carry a note from me to my wife telling her of my safety, and to bring me back tidings of her. I told him I had scarcely any money, and could only give him eight rupees; but, if he once reached my wife, I assured him she would reward him handsomely. To my great delight, he said he felt deeply for me, and would certainly do his best to convey the letter to Nynee Tal, and bring me back an answer; that he would set out the same evening for his home, arrange his affairs there, and start from thence in the morning, going through Bareilly: he had been there before and knew the way. He then retired, saying he would be back in an hour to take my letter. I sent Wuzeer Singh, who had been present at the interview, after him, to endeavour to find out whether the man was in earnest, or merely deceiving me to get the advance of money I had offered. He soon came back, saying he thought from the man's manner he could be depended on, and would certainly undertake the journey.

I determined to write two notes, one to my wife and another to Missur Byjenath at Bareilly, entreating him to aid my messenger in reaching Nynee Tal. I had but a small scrap of paper (half the fly-leaf of Bridges on the 119th Psalm, which happily we had with us,) on which to write both notes. Pen or ink I had none, and only the stump of a lead pencil, of which the lead was so nearly exhausted that only a little atom remained quite loose. I instantly commenced my writing: in the middle, the little atom of lead fell out, and I was in despair. At last, after much searching in the dust of the mud floor, I found it, and contrived to refix it in its place sufficiently to enable me to finish two very brief notes, about one inch square; which was all the man could conceal about his person, or would consent to take, as it was reported that the rebels were in the habit of searching all travellers for

together and talked with them for hours; they asking much about our country, and never ceasing in their inquiries as to how it is that our Queen's husband is not our king, which is a source of the most unfeigned surprise in them; and we inquiring of them about their cattle and habits of life, and receiving most curious information. We spent some comparatively pleasant evenings in this way with this primitive people. We also much enjoyed each evening watching the strange and interesting sight of the vast herds of cattle emerging from the jungle and swimming off in droves to their different villages, to which they seemed to direct their way with unerring instinct; the herdsman generally swimming behind them, and sometimes mounted on the stronger animals of the herd.

As the inundation was now at its height, and the waters, we knew, would equally surround Kussowrah, we were most anxious to get back to it; as we looked back upon our quarters there as palatial, compared with Runjepoorah. With this view we sent sundry messages to the Thakoors; but neither they nor Hurdeo Buksh made any sign of recognition: on the contrary, they seemed inclined to leave us to our fate. They even prohibited a poor woman, who used to attend on Mrs. Probyn and the children hitherto (and who came every morning from Kussowrah, swimming and wading, returning in the same manner of an evening), from continuing her services. This caused poor Mrs. Probyn more distress and labour than I can describe, or those imagine who were not like myself there to witness her troubles: which she bore with such patient fortitude as made me feel proud of her as my countrywoman. With the exception of this poor woman and her own ayah, Mrs Probyn had not conversed with a female since the day in which the party of Europeans left Dhurumpore to return to Futtehghur. From the Ranees of Hurdeo Buksh, or the wives of the Thakoors, influential people, and who had it in their power greatly to alleviate her position, and supply her with many comforts, she not only received no act of kindness, but no expression of sympathy whatever. To add to her already overwhelming sorrows, the poor little baby, a fine child (who, as well as the others, had up to the time we left Kussowrah continued well in spite of the exposure,) began to droop and grow daily weaker. There was no sustenance for him but buffalo's milk, which he was unable to retain; and although Probyn had left some milch goats

letters or papers, and had already killed several who were discovered with English letters on them.

When the notes were ready I got a little milk and steeped them in it, to make the writing indelible, and then put them out to dry in the sun on a wall just outside my room. In an instant a crow pounced on one and carried it off: it was that for my wife. I, of course, thought it was gone for ever, and felt heart-broken with vexation; as I had no more paper, nor any means or hope of getting any, on which to write another note. Wuzeer Singh had, unknown to me, seen the crow, followed it with one of the herdsmen, and after a long chase of about an hour, saw the bird drop it, and recovering it brought it back to me uninjured. I then despatched my messenger with both notes, and many injunctions to be deterred by no difficulties, but push his way through to Bareilly, where Byjenath would, I was certain, aid him in going on to Nynee Tal; up to this date I know not whether he has succeeded in his mission, but I think from the look of the man that he is likely to do so.

The village, which curiously enough, and surely with great truth, is known by the name of "Runjepoorah" (the place of affliction), had now become, by the constant rains and the swelling of the rivers, one complete island, of about one hundred yards square. The whole country round, as far as the eye could reach, except to the north, where there was a jungle about three miles off, was flooded; the water being in some places very deep, and nowhere under four or four and a half feet. When I step just immediately out of my own shed to go up to the Probyns, where we have our own scanty meals, the mud reaches over my ancles. Just round the village the water is very deep, and the only pasturage is about three miles distant, on the high jungle land I have mentioned, which is only partially submerged. To reach this pasture the cattle and the herdsmen have to go and return by swimming, which seems as easy and natural a mode of progression to both as travelling on dry land.

Since the waters have gone out over the country, our position is considered so much safer that we are not required to keep ourselves so strictly concealed, but are allowed to go on the roof of the house near Probyn's room, and walk about towards the afternoon. This is a great boon; and here, after sunset, when the herdsmen had returned and the cattle were folded, have we sat

of the Nana's retreating forces. The firing continued at irregular intervals for about an hour, when it entirely ceased. We remained during the day in a state of the greatest excitement, and sanguine of speedy deliverance. The day passed without Seetah Ram's return, and no tidings from any quarter reached us.

On the morning of the 24th, Seetah Ram arrived, and in reply to our eager inquiry, "Have our troops arrived? What was the firing?" he cast down our hopes by the terrible intelligence, that the firing we heard the previous morning, had been caused by the blowing away from guns, and the shooting down with grape, under the orders of the Nawab, of the poor ladies already mentioned as having been saved from the boat, and brought back to Futtehghur, and of many native Christians, in all some sixty-five or seventy persons. The Nana's soldiers, infuriated by their defeat, had, in conjunction with the Nawab, revenged themselves by the deliberate murder of these poor martyrs. Mrs. Jones's little daughter of about nine years old, Seetah Ram informed us, had remained untouched after several discharges of grape, and a sepoy rushed up and cut her in pieces with his sword.

Seetah Ram had spoken with several of the fugitive soldiers; many of them were wounded, and all were in a miserable state, from fatigue, terror, and want of food. They had with them one gun, and two or three elephants. They were completely panic-stricken, and had communicated their fears to the Nawab, and his followers. They told Seetah Ram, that the action in which they were beaten had been fought in a Nuddee between Futtehpore and Cawnpore; that the Europeans had killed numbers of them, and taken all their guns excepting the one they had with them; that it was quite in vain for them to think of contending with our troops, who used muskets (of course, the Minié), "which carried so far that they were killed before they heard the noise of the discharge." Seetah Ram also said, that such was the panic in Furrukabad, that a few persons shouting out that the Europeans were coming, had the day before nearly cleared the city; the Nawab's troops and the inhabitants all taking to flight.

The news of the success and advance of our troops caused an immediate change in the demeanour of the people towards ourselves. We received congratulatory visits from the Thakoors:

belonging to himself behind at Kussowrah, he could not induce the people to send them to him for the sustenance of his dying child.

Our position was becoming daily more deplorable, and we were prohibited from sending any of our own servants out of the village. The only person who still remained kind and visited, was the Brahmin Seetah Ram. We sent constantly messages by this man to the Thakoors; but they never took any notice of them. He had lately gone into Futtehghur for us on one or two occasions, for intelligence. This was discovered, and the Thakoors being much displeased, prohibited him from visiting us any more. The only incident which marked these weary days, was Probyn and myself, one morning, hearing distinctly a military band playing English airs in Futtehghur; the wind carrying the sound across the water, and reminding us of the near proximity of those who were, we knew, thirsting for our blood.

Early one morning, I think Thursday, the 22nd of July, when I was sitting on the roof of the house, and much depressed, my attention was attracted by seeing a person wading and swimming towards the village, and evidently desiring, by the signs he made, to catch my eye. After watching him for some time, I recognised Seetah Ram: from his manner I inferred there was something unusual. I went down to meet him as he came ashore, and found him in a great state of excitement, with the good news that our troops had at last been heard of; that they had advanced as far as Cawnpore, and had utterly defeated the Nana's troops with great slaughter at Pandoo Nuddee. The flying troops had, Seetah Ram asserted, arrived in great numbers in Furruckabad, putting the Nawab and his people in the greatest alarm that they will soon meet with the same fate; as I earnestly trust they may. I rushed up to Probyn, accompanied by Seetah Ram, to give him the welcome news; which put us in high spirits, and gave us some hopes of ultimate release.

Being, of course, most anxious to ascertain the real state of the case, we induced Seetah Ram to go across to Futtehghur, to procure intelligence. He started, promising to be back the next night. On the morning of the 23rd of July, we were startled by the firing of heavy guns in Furruckabad. We were full of hope that it was the fire of our own troops; who, we thought, might have by this time reached Futtehghur, in pursuit

whose unceasing care and devotion had been the means of keeping him alive hitherto, procured after much difficulty some hot water for a warm bath for him, which seemed to restore him; she then laid him down on a charpoy and lay down beside him. She was perfectly exhausted, having had no rest for several nights previously, during which she had to keep him in her arms, and she soon fell asleep. I was lying down at some little distance, and suddenly missing the heavy breathing, went up to the bed to look at the child: all was still, and the little spirit had fled. I woke up the parents, who, although in deep grief at losing their sweet child, felt thankful that its death had been natural, and not by the hands of assassins. We all knelt down, and prayed beside the little body; and then I went out with Wuzeer Singh, about 2 o'clock in the morning, to look for a dry spot where we might dig a grave for him. This was a matter of some difficulty, but at last we found a spot under some trees, which was not inundated, nor likely to be so. When all was prepared, the poor father took the little body wrapped in a sheet in his arms, and Mrs. Probyn followed leaning on my arm.

We had some difficulty in getting through the

cattle which were penned in the enclosure. I read a few sentences of the burial service over him. There was no time for more, as day was fast breaking and we dare not be seen beyond the village in the day-light; so we laid him in his little resting place, "dust to dust, ashes to ashes, in sure and certain hope," and hastily covered him in. I almost envied his quiet rest.

Sunday, August 2nd.—I was roused this morning before dawn by a noise in the enclosure, and on looking up saw a tall spectral looking figure standing before me, naked except a piece of cloth wrapped round his waist, much emaciated and dripping with water. I recognised him as young Mr. Jones, who, Hurdeo Buksh had informed us, had been saved from the boat captured by the Sepoys. He had until then been hidden in one of Hurdeo Buksh's villages, and, in consequence of the good news of the successful advance of our troops, had been permitted to join us. He was very weak, and when I recognised and spoke to him, burst into tears at hearing his own language again, and seeing one of his own countrymen.

The account he gave of his escape and adventures, since he left Dhurumpore, with the rest of the Europeans to return to Futtehghur, was most

old Kussuree also, whom we had not seen since we left Kussowrah, came to visit us in state on an elephant, and brought us sweet cakes, which were most acceptable. Hurdeo Buksh sent his brother-in-law to inquire after our welfare; Probyn's goats were sent to him: and the poor woman allowed to resume her attendance on Mrs. Probyn's children. In short, our position was much improved. It was not, however, quite clear, that our visitors were altogether pleased at the news of the Nana's defeat. We took advantage of this turn of feeling in our favour to entreat Hurdeo Buksh's brother-in-law to procure from him permission for us to return to Kussowrah. This request, the brother-in-law assured us, would be immediately granted, as there was now nothing to fear from the terror-stricken sepoys in Futteh-ghur.

We were particularly desirous to return, in consequence of the state of the poor little baby, who was rapidly sinking in consequence of all his hardships and exposure; and we feared that if he died in Runjepoorah, it would be impossible to get a dry spot in which to bury him; all the country around the village being flooded to a considerable depth, except the sites of the houses.

On Saturday the 26th we heard that we might return at nightfall to Kussowrah. A boat was in the afternoon sent to take off Mrs. Probyn and the children; for the waters were now deep enough between Dhurumpore and Runjepoorah. An elephant was also sent to assist in carrying us off. The Probyns went in the boat, and I and Wuzeer Singh on the elephant. This was the first time I had ever ridden one of these animals astride and bare-backed, and as we had to go through deep water and mud, half-wading, half-swimming, it was no easy task to stick on. We felt it a most blessed deliverance getting away from Runjepoorah, and were really in a state of cheerful excitement on reaching, about 9 P. M., our old quarters, where we were received by Kussuree. The place had immediately on our departure, and until within a few hours before our return, been occupied by the cattle, so our quarters were as filthy and disagreeable as when we first came to them from Dhurumpore; but filthy as they were, we looked upon them as most comfortable and commodious, after our sufferings during the previous fortnight at Runjepoorah.

The poor little baby was by this time much exhausted, and breathing very hard. His mother;

husband's grasp and immediately drowned. Robertson then put the child on his shoulder, and swam away down the stream. Jones finding that he could do no more good, wounded as he was, determined to try to save his own life by swimming down the river; hoping to reach the leading boat. As he struck out from the boat, he saw poor Mr. Fisher, the chaplain, almost in the same position as Robertson, holding his little son, a beautiful boy eight or nine years old, in one arm, while with the other he supported his wife. Mrs. Fisher was swaying about in the stream almost insensible, and her husband could with great difficulty retain his footing.

When Jones had got clear of the boat, he continued alternately swimming and floating for five or six miles, when just as it was growing dusk, he saw the leading boat anchored for the night. He reached it, much exhausted by swimming, and by the pain of his wound and of his back; which, as he was naked to the waist, had been blistered and made raw by the scorching sun. On being taken on board he found that the only casualty which had occurred to this party since leaving Futtehghur, was the death of one of the Miss Goldies, who had been killed by a grape-shot from one of the guns on the bank near Singheerampore.

Mrs. Lowis—who had maintained her fortitude throughout, and was indefatigable during the siege in preparing tea and refreshment for the men—immediately got him some brandy and water and food, and he was then able to acquaint them with the miserable fate of his own party of whom he supposed himself to be the sole survivor. The boat remained anchored in the same spot all night. Towards morning a voice was heard from the bank hailing the boat. It proved to be that of Mr. Fisher; who, though badly wounded in the thigh, had managed by swimming a portion of the way, then landing and walking along the bank, to overtake the boat. He was helped on board more dead than alive, and raved about his poor wife and son; both of whom were drowned.

At dawn they weighed anchor and proceeded down the stream; but very slowly, as there was no pilot or skilful steersman on board, and only the exhausted officers as rowers. Towards evening they became so exhausted that they made for a village on the Oude side of the Ganges, in hopes of being able to procure some milk for the children and food for themselves. The villagers brought

wonderful. They had continued to defend the fort as long as it was possible to do so; until their ammunition was almost exhausted, and the enemy's mines had rendered the place untenable. They then determined to escape in the three boats, which were held ready under the walls of the fort in case of being required. Jones happened to be in the third boat, which grounded soon after they left the fort and had to be abandoned; when he and the others on board were taken into the second boat, as already described. During the time this transfer was going on, the sepoys kept up a continual fire on the boats from their guns placed on the banks, but without doing any damage; the shot passing clear over them.

After abandoning their first boat, they managed, without loss or interruption, to get as far as the village of Singheerampore; but there their boat grounded, the villagers attacked them with matchlocks, and two guns were brought to bear on them from the bank. Jones, with the other gentlemen on board, jumped into the water to try to shove the boat off, but without any effect. While in this position, they saw a boat coming down the stream upon them; Jones jumped back into the boat to seize his rifle, which happened to be in the stern. Just as he recovered it, he saw a sepoy slowly raise the chappur (roof) of the boat and look out. Jones shot him dead; and immediately a heavy fire was opened upon them from the boat, by which Mr. Churcher, senior, a merchant, was mortally wounded. The sepoys then commenced boarding, and Jones, with most of the ladies and gentlemen, jumped into the Ganges. The last thing he saw as he quitted the boat, was poor Mr. Churcher, writhing about in his blood in the agonies of death, and Captain Fitzgerald supporting his wife on his knee, while he held a musket in his disengaged hand.

The water was up to their waists and the current running very strong: the bottom was shifting sand, which made it most difficult to maintain a footing, and several of those who took to the river were at once swept off and drowned. Jones himself had scarcely got into the water when he was hit by a musket ball, which grazed the right shoulder, without damaging the bone. At the same moment he saw Major Robertson, who was standing in the stream supporting his wife with one arm and carrying his little child in the other, wounded by a musket ball in the thigh. Mrs. Robertson was washed out of her

boat he had quitted and those in it he had no certain information. Reports had reached him similar to those we had heard, that the boat had succeeded in passing Cawnpore and reaching Allahabad in safety; again, that it had been seized near Bithoor and all on board murdered. This he, as well as we ourselves, feared was the most probable story: we strove, however, to hope for the best, and to believe that nothing so terrible could have happened.

Our morning service to-day was one of peculiar solemnity; for we knew not how soon our own fate might be the same as that of those dear friends and acquaintances so lately with us in health and vigour, and who we had too much reason to fear had all been massacred. In the midst of this depression, the reflection came upon me with a peculiar soothing and strengthening power, that the petition in the Litany—"That it might please God to succour, help, and comfort all that are in danger, necessity, and tribulation," which we knew would be offered in earnestness on this day for us by our beloved relations and friends wherever they were, and by thousands of God's servants throughout the earth—would no doubt go up with acceptance, and that we would yet be saved and be reunited to our people. The intimation also in the 11th of Hebrews, that some of God's people through faith had escaped the edge of the sword, seemed to be lit up, as it were, with a gleam of light as I read it. If they had been thus saved, why might not we hope to be so also? The arm that saved them was not shortened that it could not save us, and the ear that heard and answered their prayers was equally open and ready to receive ours, offered as they were in the name and for the sake of the same Saviour and all-powerful Advocate. Already has the promise, "I will be with him in trouble and will deliver him," been fulfilled so singularly in my own case, that surely it does not now become me to doubt. My heart was thus raised from the borders of despair to nearly an assured hope and almost to cheerfulness.

In the afternoon the man arrived whom I had sent off on the 20th of June to endeavour to take a note through Budaon to my wife at Nynee Tal. He was in a miserable plight, and told us that he had been seized at Budaon by one of my own chuprassees, Hasseinee, to whom he thought he might safely communicate the object of his journey. His confidence was sadly mis-

supplies, and did not show any ill will or attempt to attack the party.

The boat was so crowded with its freight of from seventy to eighty human beings, that Jones could find no space to lie down and sleep; he, therefore, determined, as he was quite exhausted, to go on shore and endeavour to get some rest. A villager brought him a charpoy, on which he lay down and fell fast asleep. He was roused by a summons from Colonel Smith to rejoin the boat, as they were on the point of starting; but finding himself very stiff and scarcely able to move, he determined to remain where he was, as he thought he might as well die on shore as in the boat: in either case he regarded death as inevitable. He, therefore, sent back a message that he could not come, and begged to be left behind. Colonel Smith after this sent him two more urgent requests to join the boat; which at length departed without him. He slept till morning, when a poor Brahmin took pity on him and permitted him to remain in a little shed, where he was partially sheltered from the sun. There he remained unmolested by the villagers, and protected by the Brahmin until he was permitted to join us.

His sufferings had been very great, from exposure and from his wound, which threatened mortification; this would probably have killed him had he not hit upon the following singular remedy. A little puppy came frequently to the shed when he was at his meals, to pick up any crumbs that might fall: he thought that if he could get this animal to lick the wound it might have a good effect; accordingly he made the attempt, and with the most fortunate result. The puppy licked the wound morning and evening; it at once began to improve, and was well advanced towards healing when Jones joined us.

He had left the village where he had been concealed yesterday afternoon, and by travelling all night, swimming and wading (for the whole country was under water), had reached Kussowrah just at dawn, with much difficulty. Major Robertson, he told us, was in a village about four miles from that in which he had been living, and was kindly treated. Mr. Churcher, junior, was in an Aheer village at a considerable distance from either his or Robertson's place of hiding. None of them had been permitted to see or communicate with one another.

Such was Jones's account of himself. Of the

we hear, is still holding out, and some of our troops from Cawnpore have, it is said, advanced to the relief of the garrison. May God grant them success.

Tuesday, August 4th.—I was walking up and down the little space in front of our room to-day, when I was rejoiced by the arrival of my messenger Rohna from Nynee Tal, with a letter from my wife of the 27th July; the first I have had from her since the 26th of May. Rohna had seen both her and Gracey quite well. He told me that she was dressed in black when he reached the house, and that when she received my letter she had gone away and put on a white dress.

Before opening the note, which was, of course, of the smallest dimensions, I went into my little room to bless God for his great goodness in granting me this great comfort. On opening the letter I read, with deep thankfulness, not only of her own and my child's safety, but also of that of my brother Roderick and his wife at Mozuffernugger; of which he had been appointed Collector immediately after the Meerut outbreak. He has been able to hold his own, and maintain to some extent the peace of the district, by means of a force of 60 Gorkhas and some Affghan Horse placed at his disposal.

Her note confirms the news which had reached

me before, but I hoped was not true, of the murder of poor Hay, Robertson, and Raikes at Bareilly, and of the Shahjehanpore massacre. By her account Nynee Tal is quite safe, also Agra; and Delhi, though not taken, is likely to fall. The Punjaub and all down to Meerut quite quiet. This was the first authentic intelligence we had received of the real state of affairs in the North-West since the 13th of June, and we were much comforted by finding that matters were not quite so bad as the Thakoors had made us believe.

Rohna told us that he had experienced the greatest difficulty in getting through Bareilly and on to the hills, as all travellers were strictly searched for letters at different posts of the rebels along the road. He had concealed mine to my wife in the interior of a bamboo walking-stick, and knowing that this would be most likely seized and examined, he cracked it across half-way up, so that if taken from him and broken, it might give way at that exact part, and the portion in which the letter was concealed remain sound and escape detection.

This actually occurred. He was stopped at a post between Bareilly and Rampore by a soldier, who took the stick from him, struck one end on the

placed, for he was instantly seized and conveyed before the Nawab who was governing the district for Khan Bahadoor Khan. My letter was taken from him; he was beaten and imprisoned; for twelve days he was kept in confinement and treated with great severity; and at last allowed to depart only on his pledging himself never again to act as a messenger for any European. Being released, he determined to come back to me; he had arrived within about twenty miles of Furruckabad, when he was arrested by a guard of the Nawab's troops as a spy of the English, and sent into Furruckabad, where he was detained in prison, with several others, for three weeks. On the afternoon of yesterday he was released by the man in charge of the prison; whom he bribed with eight annas, all he had in the world.

Just before he left Futtehghur, he had seen three persons who had been seized with English letters on them, which they were conveying from Agra down the country, blown away from guns on the parade ground, by order of the Nawab. He described the state of the town and district of Budaon, and of all the other British districts he had passed through, as deplorable in the extreme. Villages were being burnt and plundered daily;

the roads deserted, and no man's life or property was safe for a moment. In Budaon itself there had been some fighting between the Mahommedans and Hindoos, and he saw a number of heads of persons of the latter exposed on poles at the entrance of the town.

All my police and native Amlah were in the service of Khan Bahadoor Khan; my old Foujdarry Serishtadar (head clerk in the criminal department) was Magistrate of Budaon, and my Kotwal held the same appointment under the rebels. I am much surprised at the defection of these two men; both excellent officers, who have served the British Government for at least forty years with credit to themselves and advantage to the State, and were about to retire on handsome pensions. My messenger said that while our districts were thus subject to fire and sword, those in Oude under the talookdars and powerful zemindars were calm and peaceful as a lake. This is certainly the case with the extensive talooqua of Hurdeo Buksh, and those of powerful chiefs immediately around us. The rebellion has not as yet extended to these estates; the people go about their usual avocations, and all is quiet and peaceful within their limits. Lucknow,

an opportunity of returning to Rohilcund. Heard from the Thakoors that the reinforcements from Cawnpore had reached Lucknow. They had a fight, *en route* in which the enemy suffered most severely; a chief called Jessah Singh was wounded, and one of his sons killed. The result of this success to us was a great increase of politeness, and the permission granted to take a walk last night.

How true do I now find the remark I remember once reading of Arnold's, that "the Psalms have been a storehouse of never-failing comforts to believers in every age." Since our return from Runjpoorah, Mrs. Probyn has received a box of her things, which had been in Hurdeo Buksh's keeping at Dhurumpore. Among the contents was her Bible; and, oh! what a comfort has it been to us since, as we are thereby enabled to read the Psalms. There is not a day on which we do not find something that appears as if written especially for persons in our unhappy circumstances, to meet the feelings and wants of the day. This morning, for instance, I derived unspeakable comfort from the 15th and 20th verses of the 25th Psalm, and in the evening from verses 5, 6, 7, 12, 13, 14 of the 27th Psalm.

Thursday, August 6th.—No news yet to-day. We shall probably now have evil reports; as of late, they have been unusually favourable. This has been a day of much depression and faintness of heart. Help seems so far off, and rescue so improbable, that fears constantly arise that I shall one day perish in my affliction, and never again on earth see those so dear to me. If this be God's will, and if this little journal ever reaches my beloved wife, children, and all at home, it may interest them to see how I spent my day, and where we live, so I shall endeavour to draw a plan of the place.

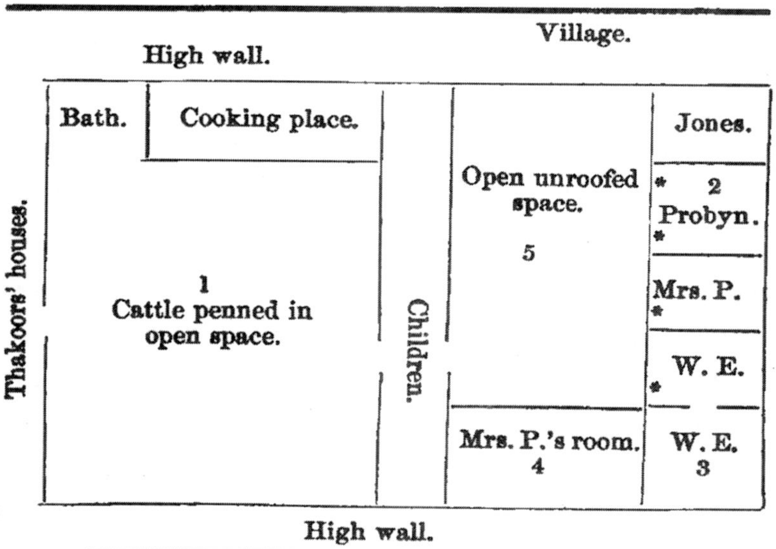

* Verandah where we slept and dined.

ground, breaking it in half as was intended, and then, thinking it contained nothing, threw the pieces away; Rohna picked them up again, and proceeded on his way without further notice. My wife's letter for me he had sewn up in the lining of his skull-cap, which had more than once on the road been taken from his head by sepoys; but without the note being discovered. I sent Wuzeer Singh to tell Hurdeo Buksh, that I had good news from my wife, who gave favourable intelligence of the state of things in the country to the north of us. He sent back many congratulations and kind messages, with the news which had just reached that the boat full of Futtehghur refugees had reached Allahabad in safety, and that Agra had been reinforced by three European and two Sikh regiments. If this be true, we may hope that Delhi has fallen; for from no other quarter could the reinforcements come. The heat to-day was terrible.

Wednesday, August 5th.—Last evening, for the first time since our first arrival at Kussowrah, we have been allowed to go out to take a walk; as the waters completely surround the village, and there is no danger of any spies or strangers arriving and seeing us. The change was most refreshing, from our miserable little pent-up quarters to the open country. Everything looked peaceful; the people were at their usual occupations; there were no external signs that war and rebellion were raging all around us, and that we ourselves were as "the hunted partridge on the mountains," with but a step between us and death, and that in a fearful form.

To-day I sent off a man of Byjenath's, who had accompanied Rohna from Bareilly, with another letter for my wife. He made strong objections to taking any, on account of the great risk of detection; which would result in certain death. He could only be induced to do so when I put my note into a piece of quill about this size (   ) sealed at each end, which he could carry in his mouth, and swallow in the event of being stopped.

I learnt from this man that the Mahomedans had begun persecuting the Hindoos in Rohilcund, slaying cows in the temple and prohibiting their sounding their 'sonks' (horns). The Thakoors had, in consequence, summoned the people to assemble and attack their persecutors. If they answer the summons, the Hindoos, from their superior numbers, may expel the other sect; and in that event the Europeans may have

missionary at a festival, and had treasured carefully ever since. He lent this copy to us, and I read portions of it daily with Wuzeer Singh. About 5 o'clock I manage to get a bathe in the cattle-shed just beyond our dwelling. By the time we are dressed the shadows of evening are lengthening, and we have our dinner in the verandah; the charpoys (our beds) being our only tables as well as seats. This meal generally consists of a little rice, chupatties, and a watery kind of native vegetable, something like cucumber, stewed; sometimes we are fortunate enough to purchase a kid or lamb, and then have a sumptuous dinner on chops, but this is rare. At Runjpoorah we could procure no meat or rice, and lived on a kind of chupatties called poorees, and tea or buffalo's milk. This poor food made us all, especially the children, thin and weak. Our meal is soon discussed, and then we sit and talk together, or go out and have a chat with the Thakoors while the cattle are being milked. As soon as it grows dark we have prayers and go to bed, as we have no lights, and cannot better employ ourselves.

Our sleep is, of course, much broken, for our senses have become so acute from constant watchfulness, that the slightest unusual noise, even the movement of a bird on the trees close to us, is sufficient to awake and make us start up. At present scarcely a night passes that we do not hear the sound of heavy guns at a great distance in the Lucknow direction, which we suppose to be the fire of the besiegers on the Residency.

Thus our days pass, sometimes diversified by the receipt of favourable, at others, and, indeed for the most part, of very dreadful and alarming rumours, most trying and distressing to persons in our position. The inactivity is so hard to bear: we can do nothing to improve our position, but merely await the progress of events as patiently as we can. In the morning we feel inclined to say, would God it were evening; and in the evening, would God it were morning.

Saturday, August 8th.—Just as I supposed, we have unpleasing accounts this morning, to counterbalance the favourable ones that have reached us for the past few days. Lucknow is said to have fallen: "to be empty," as the Thakoors' expression is. May God forbid! I don't think it is probable.

Another report is that two regiments of our Irregular Cavalry, who had joined the Nana and were among his defeated troops which had arrived

I wake at the first sign of dawn, about 4 A.M., at once get up; and, after prayer, go out to walk in the space marked 1, as soon as the cattle who occupy it all night are let out. It is an open space about thirty or forty yards long, where we are allowed to walk morning and evening. I thus try and get a little exercise; or sit down upon a log and read the Morning Psalms until the sun gets too hot. I am then driven into my little den marked 3, where Wuzeer Singh always places my charpoy as soon as I get up.

Thus the time passes until we judge by the sun that it is about 10 o'clock, when we read the Scriptures and have prayers together. We then have breakfast, which consists of chupatties and tea; of which, fortunately for us, we have a large supply. The box containing it belonged to poor Robert Thornhill, and was left behind at Dhurumpore when he returned to Futtehghur.

The heat, glare, and flies, which come around us now in myriads, are most distressing and well nigh intolerable. To escape the two last plagues, I generally resort to my little room, which I darken by hanging my blanket across the opening, as there is no door. The atmosphere within is quite stifling, but I prefer breathing it to remaining outside, as the glare hurts my eyes. I then employ myself in reading the Scriptures and that excellent book Bridges on the 119th Psalm; of which Mrs. Probyn had a copy in her box, lately received from Dhurumpore, as well as her Bible. Up to my return to Kussowrah from Runjpoorah, I had only my little Testament; but Mrs. Probyn now lends me her Bible for some hours daily, when not requiring it herself. What a blessing it is to us having the Scriptures with us! I have no books and no other employment than studying them; and what a source of real substantial comfort and support they are! But, alas! the bitter thought constantly occurs "For you these lessons how to lead a Christian life are no longer applicable; you have now but to study how to meet death like a Christian." About 3 o'clock Wuzeer Singh comes in daily, and I read a portion of Scripture and pray with him in Hindustani.

Some weeks since, before we left for Runjpoorah, I inquired of the Thakoors if they had any books in Hindee, as I wished to amuse myself by reading them; the only one in their possession was a copy of St. Luke's Gospel, which one of them had received some years before from a

at Futtehghur, had gone off to Cawnpore to endeavour to be re-employed by us; being enraged by the conduct towards them of the Furrukabad Nawab, who caused them to be plundered of two elephants and other property, and, telling them he did not require their services, would have nothing to do with them.

The Thakoors made a proposal to me this morning to convey me to Nynee Tal, *viâ* Phillibheet. Kussuree had a daughter married to a powerful Thakoor, near Phillibheet; she died leaving a little daughter, who has been living for some time with her grandfather, and is now about to return to her father. She is to be conveyed in a covered palanquin, and it is proposed that I am to be concealed within, travelling all night with this child, and halting during the day in the houses of friends, where I would be safe from detection. In the event of being stopped on the march, the child was immediately to be shown; which it was expected would at once remove suspicion and allow of our passing unmolested. From the Thakoors' house I was to be sent on by Kussuree to the foot of the hills, what they call "Teehun Teehun;" that is, from friend's house to friend's house, all pledged to secrecy. The plan seems possible. May God prosper it, if it is likely to be for good; or if not, defeat it. Probyn's opinion is most strong against all attempt to escape by any other course than down the Ganges.

Sunday, August 9th.—Not so peaceful a Sunday as we could wish; our minds are cast down and distracted by many rumours of our want of success at Cawnpore, and of weakness everywhere.

Probyn had some days ago, by the advance of twenty rupees, induced a man (a relation of Seeta Ram) to try and reach Cawnpore, and bring us news from thence; giving him a letter to the commanding officer, whoever he might be. This man returned to-day saying that the place was so closely beleaguered by the Nana's troops all around it, that he could not get nearer cantonments than nine miles; and that he had been so hard pressed that, to escape detection, he had hidden the letter he carried under the root of a tree, where he had left it. Lucknow, he reported, had been taken and the garrison put to the sword; and that Cawnpore must soon, from the numbers investing it, be destroyed in like manner. To prove that he had actually been as far as he stated, he brought us a piece of the telegraph wire. By a little cross-examination, however, we discovered that he had never attempted the journey, but had remained all the time of his supposed absence quietly in his house, in his village about fifteen miles off. Seeta Ram was so exasperated at the conduct of his relation, whom he had recommended to us, that he volunteered to convey a note for us himself to Cawnpore, whenever we might wish to send him.

Monday, August 10th.—Despatched Rohna with a little note in a quill for my wife. He is to go to Phillibheet, and endeavour to arrange for my journey from thence to Nynee Tal; and to bring back news to me whether the road is practicable.

He had scarcely been gone two hours when Missur Byjenath's man, Khan Singh, who had previously visited me, arrived. I immediately sent for him, confident that he had brought me a letter from Nynee Tal. Much, however, was I disappointed to find that he had not been there, and only came from Bareilly, charged by his master to see how I was getting on, and to ascertain the exact posture of affairs at Cawnpore. I was so vexed at getting no letter, that I could hardly speak to him or listen to his news; which, however, was rather satisfactory. Our troops before Delhi were, he states, most successful. Meerut and Saharunpore, and the Hill stations, were quite safe. Khan Bahadoor Khan's army, he describes as most contemptible, unarmed and ill-disciplined, and having only six guns of small calibre. The report of troops reaching Futtehghur would be quite enough, he assured us, to clear Rohilcund of rebels, and restore it to the British; as the Hindoos were on our side, and were burning to revenge themselves on the Mahomedans.

We had all, as well as the Thakoors, been present at this conference with Khan Singh. At its close I dismissed Khan Singh, saying I would let him go the next day with a letter for Byjenath, and one for Nynee Tal. As he was rising to go away, he made a secret sign to me, unobserved by the others, showing that he wished to say something to me in private. I took the hint, and half an hour after, and when I was alone in my own room, I sent Wuzeer Singh to bring him back.

He then told me that his master, thinking, that if I was alive, I must be hard pressed for money, had sent me 500 rupees (50*l.*) for my expenses. It was contained in two "hoondees" (bills), drawn on a banker at Goorsehain Gunj, near Cawnpore, nominally, in order to deceive any parties who might seize him and take them from him, but really payable, through a secret cipher, by a banker in Furrukabad. Khan Singh said he could easily make his way into that place. The story he had told along the road, and which he intended to repeat to the sepoys if seized by them there, was this: that before the disturbances, his master had sent off a boat laden with indigo seed under care of his own people to Cawnpore; that this boat had not been heard of for three months, and as the people must be in great want of money, his master had sent him with these hoondees to cash at Goorsehain Gunj, and provide for their expenses, if he could hear of and find them.

All this is easy enough, Khan Singh said: the sepoys would not interfere with him, so long as he had only hoondees; which would be useless to them. The real difficulty would be, to get the money back safe after the bills were cashed; how to accomplish this, he knew not. Wuzeer Singh suggested that we should consult with old Kussuree on the subject; who, he was certain, could be trusted, and was a shrewd safe man: none of the others he assured us could be confided in. If they once knew that I had 500 rupees, they might get rid of me in order to possess themselves of the money; the whole matter must therefore be kept a profound secret from all but Kussuree.

I told him that, when it was dark, and Kussuree had gone to rest, he had better speak to him, and try to arrange some plan. The old man always slept in a place by himself, beside a favourite mare and foal of his; so the conference was sure to be secret.

We had gone to bed early, as it was a dark rainy tempestuous night, when I was awoke by Mrs. Probyn starting up from her charpoy exclaiming, "There is the Bheestie!" I started up and saw a man just entering the enclosure. This was Probyn's water-carrier, whom a fortnight or three weeks before he had despatched to Agra with a letter to Reade, his uncle, telling him of our position, and requesting information and advice. We all then jumped up, and eagerly demanded his news, and if he had got a letter for us. He said he had, enclosed in his stick, a heavy bamboo. The note was so ingeniously and securely secreted, and the stick so hard, that it took us more than half an hour to get at it. It was in the Greek character, and gave us most welcome news: that all was well at Agra, since an action they had fought in July, when they had to retire into the fort; that our troops were pretty successful at Delhi, heating back with ease all sallies of the mutineers; that the China troops had reached Calcutta; and that General Havelock was coming up to relieve Lucknow, and had probably done so by that time. For ourselves he recommended us to remain where we were, until a safe opportunity offered of our getting into the British camp at Cawnpore.

He did not anticipate that our forces would recapture Futtehghur for a long time to come. The only unsatisfactory part of Reade's information was that the Gwalior Contingent had mutinied and was threatening Agra; but as the Chumbul river was in full flood they could not cross it for some time, and in the meantime Agra was safe.

Tuesday, August 11th.—Notwithstanding the news of last night this was a day of unusual gloom and depression. Reports reached us which were fully believed by the Thakoors—who are, of course, always ready to give credit to sinister rumours, and never to any in our favour—that Cawnpore is completely surrounded by the rebels; that our troops have been beaten and obliged to raise the siege of Delhi; that General Havelock's force had failed to relieve the Lucknow garrison and had been driven back to Cawnpore; also that a proclamation had arrived from the Begum at Lucknow, offering a reward of a thousand rupees for each of our heads, to any one who would bring them in.

The Thakoors plainly told us that the arrival of this proclamation had greatly increased the danger of our position; for that now it would be an object for any of the villagers to take our lives, as the party would be worth to them 4,000 or 5,000 rupees. They urged us never to show ourselves in daylight in the little enclosure outside our rooms, and to keep a strict watch at night; to be careful to close the entrance, and have our guns and pistols always ready beside us. Things certainly looked very gloomy.

In the evening Hurdeo Buksh visited us, and plainly told us, he feared he could keep us no longer; that I ought at once to start for Nynee Tal, or go with the Probyns, whom he intended to send down by land to Cawnpore. He had, he said, sent down some of his people to endeavour to arrange for our safe conduct through Oude, by passing us on from one friend's house to another friend's house, into General Havelock's camp. He had received favourable replies from several of his friends on the line, and only awaited answers from one or two others. Jussah Singh he said, had professed his willingness to receive us, and pass us on safe into the British camp.

Probyn expressed his great dissatisfaction at this part of the proposal; saying it was well known that Jussah Singh was a confederate of Nana Sahib, who was in hiding at his place of Futtehpore Chowrassee; and that besides, Jussah Singh had been wounded when fighting against us. Hurdeo Buksh allowed that this was the case, but said that there was no fear, as Jussah Singh had pledged his honour for our safety to him, and a Rajpoot was never known to break his pledged word to a fellow chief. Go, however, he said, we must, whatever objection we had; for as soon as the Lucknow garrison fell (an event which probably had already taken place) the Aumils would be sent all over the country with troops, and every avenue of escape would be closed to us. He then left us, saying he would let us know as soon as final arrangements had been made for our land journey.

This determination of Hurdeo Buksh to send us off, and the opinion expressed by Reade, that it was by no means probable that Futtehghur would soon be retaken by our troops, and that consequently our only chance of escape was to get into the British camp at Cawnpore, made us most anxious to communicate with General Havelock; who, we learnt for the first time from Reade's communication, was commanding there. We therefore determined to avail ourselves of Seetah Ram's offer to go to Cawnpore, and to send him with a letter, which Probyn wrote in Greek characters, to Havelock, and enclosed in a quill, telling the General of our desperate situation, and asking his advice how best to attempt our escape to join his camp.

Seetah Ram is to start on his mission early to-morrow morning, and we hope may return in eight or ten days; the inundation, however, is so wide spread, that he does not expect to cross the Ganges until to-morrow night. This morning Wuzeer Singh informed me, that he had in the night sounded Kussuree about the best way of conveying the money from Furrukabad, and that he and Khan Singh would come in the evening and talk it over—which they did about 5 o'clock in the afternoon. Kussuree proposed that two ponies should be hired from a neighbouring village beyond Hurdeo Buksh's domain; as any from one of his villages would be liable to be stopped, and seized at the Ghauts on the Ganges by the

Nawab's people. These ponies were to be brought to Kussowrah, there laden with grain, and taken into Furrukabad, as if to dispose of their loads. The Nawab's people and the sepoys were anxious to encourage supplies being brought into the city, and would not interfere with them. When the loads were sold, the ponies were to be taken at nightfall to the house of the banker who was to cash the bills, and the money would then be sewn into their pack-saddles. Next morning the animals would be taken across the river, and being apparently merely on their return home unladen would not probably be suspected or stopped. This appeared to me as good a plan as could be adopted; and Wuzeer and Khan Singh are to go in the morning to some villages about eight miles off to hire the ponies: being strangers and not known to the people, they will not be suspected.

Thursday, August 13th.—Last night we were made happy by hearing that Cawnpore had been reinforced by eight regiments: of course, this is the China force just arrived, and in the very nick of time. All may now be repaired. Soon after, we were depressed by the report, given by sepoy returning to his home, who halted for a short time in the village, that fifteen mutinous regiments from Bombay had arrived at Gwalior. Of these eight had crossed the Chumbul to reinforce the rebels at Delhi, and the rest had remained in Gwalior, to join in the attack on Agra with Scindiah's Contingent as soon as the season permits. Another report has reached us, that Oude has been restored to its King. I would rejoice in such an equitable measure at another time; but at present, if it be true, which I cannot believe, it is a sign of a falling cause, and of great and deplorable weakness. Heard also that Delhi had been without doubt abandoned by our troops, who were forced to retreat and are probably besieged themselves in turn. All these reports, added to great heat and swarms of mosquitoes, made me pass a miserable, almost a terrific night; fancying that, if Delhi had been abandoned, the Gorkhas must have deserted us, and Nynee Tal, in that case, be in extreme danger, if it had not already fallen, and all Europeans in it massacred.

Our general defence against mosquitoes is to light each night some dried cow-dung in the corner of the place where we sleep, to windward; and the thick smoke being carried over our beds during the night, drains off these insects. Last night, however, this resource failed us, for there was not a breath of air, and the smoke from the burning fuel hung so thick and heavy about us, that we could not breathe, and had to extinguish the fire. The mosquitoes, of course, taking advantage of the opportunity, fell upon us in myriads, and rendered sleep or rest nearly impracticable.

It is impossible to describe the depression of mind and body which follows nights of this kind. It is at such times I feel the real blessing the Psalms are. They never fail to give peace and refreshment, when all is dark and gloomy within and without. The circumstances under which many of them were written, seasons of danger and almost despair—David fleeing and hiding from bloodthirsty enemies, as we are—render them peculiarly suitable to our case. This morning I felt the 5th verse of the 68th Psalm most soothing, in the assurance it gives me that if I am cut off, my God will be with my widow and fatherless children. Again, the fact asserted in the following verse, that God "setteth the solitary in families," is most comforting. Unto Him belong the issues of life and death, and He may be pleased to show forth His power even for me the most unworthy of His servants, and restore me to my family.

Friday, August 14th.—Strange rumours to-day that the Governor-General with the King of Oude will reach Cawnpore this day, and that on their arrival Oude is to be formally made over to its ancient ruler. The Thakoors seem quite delighted at the prospect, and say the orders have come from the "English council at home," meaning the Court of Directors, "who always do justice." They often speak to me about the annexation, and ask me why the Governor-General acted on "Sullivan Sahib's" advice, as they call Sleeman; who, they assert, was the man who ruined their "raj."

They speak with the greatest respect and affection of some of our officers, especially of Christian, late Commissioner at Singapore, and swear vengeance against the Dobusiees (the 41st) who murdered him and his family at that place. If they could always have got access to him, they say, they would have had no reason to complain of our administration; but he had too much to do, and was seldom visible. The native officials they describe as regular harpies, and a native deputy-collector who had been stationed at Sandee, they frequently mention to me with expressions of the deepest hatred. This fellow, they assert, had a pair of slippers of extra size made, on purpose for "shoe beating" (the most disgraceful punishment that can be inflicted on a native) in open Kutcherry any one who refused to pay him what he demanded in the shape of bribes, or to sign any agreements respecting the disposal of their villages or land that he chose to fix upon, however unjust and ruinous to their interests these might be. Old Kussuree told me that he had paid a thousand rupees in petitions alone, not one of which ever reached Christian, and more than 6,000 rupees in bribes; notwithstanding which he had lost the villages farmed by him and his ancestors for many generations, and had been assessed so highly for those he had left, that he had only been able to pay his rent the preceding year by the sale of some of his family jewels and a mare he highly valued; and this year he said he would no doubt have been a defaulter, and been sold up, had not the bulwah (rebellion) fortunately occurred.

I asked him why he did not go to Lucknow and complain in person to the Chief Commissioner. He replied that he had made one journey to Lucknow in the King's time, with some petition about his villages, and it so nearly cost him his life, that he would never enter that city again. "I was then," he said, "a fine powerful man, 'khoob inwan,' and passed my way into the King's presence in open durbar, armed in the usual way, and as we all are in these parts, with my sword, shield, and matchlock. I was unaware of the rules of the Court, which forbid armed men to enter the durbar, and had left the match of my matchlock burning. The King caught sight of it alight, and rushed out of durbar, crying out, 'Seize and kill him: he wants to assassinate me!' I was instantly pinioned, and carried off to be blown from a gun. No one would listen to my expostulations, as I was a stranger; and it was believed that I had been caught in the act of attempting to murder the King. Most fortunately for me, as I was being carried off, an officer met the party, and stopped it to look at the prisoner. He was from these parts, and an old friend of mine. He recognised me and cried out, 'Kussuree Singh is no traitor, but an honest zemindar of high character; there must be some mistake.' I then told him how, by my allowing the match of my gun to remain alight, I had got into this trouble, which was likely to cost me my life. He had influence enough to stop my execution until he could communicate with the authorities, and on his explanation I was ordered to be released. I left Lucknow that night, have never seen it since, and never will again, with my will."

In the conversations I have had with Hurdeo Buksh, who is a very superior intelligent man, he has given me to understand that the native Omlahs,* who were introduced in such shoals into Oude immediately after the annexation, were the curse of the country, and in his plain-spoken phrase, "made our rule to stink in the nostrils of the people." Of Christian and many other officers he spoke in terms of high commendation and respect. He never hesitated, he said, to go to Christian, who always treated him (as Probyn had invariably, at Futtehghur,) as a gentleman, gave him a seat, and conversed with him with affability; but to any *native* official under Government he declared he would as soon lose his life as go.

Tuesday, August 18th. — This evening Khan Singh returned with the money all safe from Furrukabad. The ponies, which had been hired by Wuzeer Singh and him, were duly laden at Kussowrah, and driven to a ghaut on the Ganges, where they crossed. Khan Singh went in the

* Civil officers of Government employed in collecting revenue.

same boat, but did not ostensibly have any connection with them. The ponies were allowed to pass with their loads, as soon as the guard at the ghaut ascertained that they did not belong to any of Hurdeo Buksh's villages. Khan Singh was, on landing, seized and brought before the Subahdar in command. He exhibited his hoondees, told the story he had prepared beforehand—that he had been sent by his master to make advances to the boat's crew belonging to him—and expressed his confidence that, as it was the object of the sepoys not to hurt but to foster honest traders, they would not interfere with, or detain him. The Subahdar believed his story, wished him success, and dismissed him. The ponies' loads were disposed of in the Bazaar, and the animals themselves taken at nightfall secretly to the bankers, where the money was sewn into their pack-saddles. Next morning at dawn, their drivers drove them back across the ghaut unquestioned; Khan Singh, to avoid recognition, recrossing himself at a ghaut some miles higher up the Ganges. He rejoined them on this side, and they all arrived safely at Kussowrah. And now, through the noble conduct of Missur Byjenath—who, without any solicitation of mine has of his own accord advanced me money, at a time when my life is by no means secure and repayment is most uncertain—and the cool intrepidity and intelligence of his servant, I am supplied with as much cash as I can possibly require, and placed above want.

On receiving the money, my first desire was to pay Wuzeer Singh some wages, as he had received no pay since leaving his regiment in February. He refused to receive one cowrie, saying, "When I see you seated in kutcherry again, I will take pay: until then I can support myself well enough with the balance of my pay." Nothing could move him from his determination. I was afraid to keep the money myself, so I made it over to Kussuree to retain for me.

Thursday, August 20th.—Nothing has occurred since last entry worthy of note. To-day a messenger was sent to us from Hurdeo Buksh, to say that a man had arrived at Dhurumpore, asking for Probyn, and that he had him detained as a spy. Probyn begged that the man might be sent on to us. He soon after arrived, and turned out to be a messenger from Deighton Probyn from Delhi, which place he had only left nine days before. The letter was sewn up in the sole of the man's shoe, and had to be cut out. It was of course much soiled, but quite legible, and informed us that all was going on favourably at Delhi, and the insurgents were losing heart from continual defeats. The messenger informs us that he had seen numbers of sepoys on the road, returning to their homes with their plunder. He had met one man on a camel, who gave out in the villages as he came along, that the British army had been cut to pieces in his presence, and the Emperor had sent him down express to announce the happy tidings to the Nawab of Furrukabad. Probyn's messenger inquired of this man when he had left Delhi; and on hearing that he had started two days before himself, knew that his statement was quite false, and remonstrated with him for propagating such falsehoods. The man replied that he was carrying home plenty of plunder, and gave himself out to be an imperial messenger to save himself from being stopped and plundered by the villagers.

Seetah Ram returned this evening from Cawnpore: but, to our bitter mortification, without any note from General Havelock in reply to Probyn's. Seetah Ram had safely reached the British camp, and falling in with some Sikhs, was conducted by them to General Havelock's tent; when he delivered his letter, and was told to wait for an answer. This he did for the whole of the next day, but received none. The second morning the force moved out towards Bithoor, and Seetah Ram accompanied General Havelock's servants with the force. A battle was fought about midday, in which the insurgents were beaten with much slaughter. Seetah Ram was present throughout, and states that the fire of our artillery was so terrific, that it was impossible for the enemy to stand against it for a moment. After the action he tried to get speech of the General, but he was too busy to attend to him. Next day, General Havelock moved to attack a body of the enemy which had retreated to some place near Sheorajpore, where he beat them again soundly. The order was then given to return to Cawnpore, and Seetah Ram, fearing we might be much disappointed by the delay in his return, and thinking there was no hope of getting any reply from the General, started on his return, and reached us in due course. His news was good and most cheering; but his mission, as we told him, had been useless, as he had brought us no reply from the General. As Havelock is an old friend of mine,

I have thought it best to write to him myself, and entreat of him to send us some reply. Seetah Ram is to start with this letter to-morrow.

Friday, August 21st.—Poor Probyn's little girl died this morning: she had drooped ever since the exposure and privations of Runjpoorah, and ever since our return had gradually grown weaker, notwithstanding her mother's increasing care and watchfulness: another victim to these sad troubles; as, in all human probability, had the child not been subjected to such hardships, or even if medical aid or medicines had been available, she would have lived. When I joined the party at Dhurumpore, she was a fine, healthy, and very pretty child, with beautiful hair thickly curling over her head. As soon as it was dusk, we went out and dug a grave, and at midnight carried out the little body wrapped in a sheet, and buried her by her little brother. I can never forget her parents' agony. She had been a favourite child, and to see her wasting away daily and suffering from disease, without being able to administer anything for her relief, was almost too distressing to bear. But it is God's will, and what we know not now we shall know hereafter.

Saturday, August 22nd.—I sent off Seetah Ram

this morning with my note to General Havelock, desiring him to make all speed in returning, as the good effects of the late success in opening the roads might soon wear away. Hurdeo Buksh called upon us in the forenoon of to-day, for the first time at this hour since we have been in this place: he generally chose the dead of night for his visits. He was in high spirits in consequence of Havelock's successful advance and the intelligence which had reached him of reinforcements pouring into Cawnpore. Not one of the Talookdars or men of influence in Oude, he asserted, had yet joined the rebels, with the exception of Jussah Singh; who had been reported dead of his wounds. Hurdeo Buksh tells us that he has received a copy of a proclamation, issued by the Subahdars in command of the mutineers at Delhi and Lucknow, to all the chief landowners in Oude. In this document they express their surprise and sorrow that, although the army had risen in defence of their religion and for the common good, the landowners had not co-operated with the soldiers, or given them the aid they counted upon when they rose. In consequence of their backwardness, the army now found themselves unable to contend successfully against the

British; the Subahdars, therefore, thought it right to warn all the chief men of influence and rank in Oude that it was the intention of the British, as soon as they had destroyed the army, to collect all the high-caste men and sweepers in the province at one enormous feast, and make them all eat together. The Subahdars, therefore, thought it their duty to give the chiefs fair warning of the intentions of the British Government, and to entreat them, for the sake of their common faith, to aid the army with their forces, and to rise and exterminate the infidels, and avoid so fearful a catastrophe as the loss of their caste.

Hurdeo Buksh said, "You and I know that this is all nonsense and folly; but the proclamation is a highly dangerous and inflammable document, for its contents are implicitly believed by the common people, who are consequently much exasperated against the English."

His own relations and tenantry, he says, have become in consequence highly displeased with him for harbouring us; and this ill-feeling has been much aggravated by the Nawab and Subahdar in Futtehghur having issued orders to prevent any people from his villages crossing the Ganges, or getting any supplies from Furrukabad of salt, sugar, and other necessaries hitherto procured from thence. The result of this deprivation is that the people are becoming excited to a degree highly dangerous to us, and Hurdeo Buksh fears he cannot much longer restrain them. Besides all this, the inundation was, he observed, daily diminishing, and he had always told us that the moment the waters subsided his power to protect us would be at an end. He, therefore, thought we should, with reference to all these circumstances, make up our minds to endeavour to escape by the river to Cawnpore; and to start without loss of time, while the recent successes of our troops were fresh in the minds of the people, and the route was comparatively safe. He had ordered a boat to be prepared for us, and as soon as it was ready he should start us off. We told him that we quite coincided in his opinion, that it was now high time to attempt to escape by the river; and that we would be ready to start on the return of the messenger we had sent to Cawnpore, who might be expected in a few days with a reply from General Havelock. Hurdeo Buksh was satisfied with this, and left us.

Sunday, August 23rd.—We had for some days

made our projected attempt to escape by the Ganges the repeated subject of prayer, together and by ourselves, for guidance as to what course we should pursue, and that God would in mercy be pleased to open a way of escape for us. I went into my room this morning to look up the lessons for the day before meeting for prayers, when turning over the Bible, I was much struck by coming upon the 8th chapter, verses 21, 22, 23, and 31, of the book of Ezra; which seemed so peculiarly suitable to our circumstances as to be quite startling. I read the passage to the Probyns, and we were by this little incident so much strengthened and encouraged that we feel now little or no hesitation in undertaking our perilous journey.

Monday, 24th.—Sinister rumours are rife to-day in the village, and of course are duly communicated to us, that the insurgents are again re-assembling in the neighbourhood of Cawnpore, and have attacked and expelled the police from the re-established stations. It is also reported that Ranee Chunda Koonwur, mother of Dhuleep Singh, has effected her escape from Nepaul, and has arrived at Futtehghur, *en route* to the Punjaub. If this be true, and she succeeds in reaching her destination, the consequences may be most troublesome, if not disastrous.

Finished to-day, for the second time, that excellent work Bridges on 119th Psalm; the sole book in my hands, except the Bible, for the past two months: and fortunate have I been to have had these sources of consolation. I found great comfort and encouragement to-day in reading his remarks on faith, in his commentary on the 116th verse; which contains, I think, the real scriptural doctrine. However our own frames may change, or our power of comprehension vary, He remains the same, yesterday, to-day, and for ever: we can neither add to nor detract anything from the completeness of His finished work.

Just as we were falling off asleep last night we were aroused by the arrival of a messenger from General Havelock. We jumped up, eager to get his expected communication; but, to our bitter disappointment, found that he had only brought a letter from the General to Hurdeo Buksh, commending him for his humanity and loyalty in having protected us hitherto, and assuring him of high rewards if he would send us safe into the British camp, as soon as it reached Futtehghur.

The messenger quite raised our spirits by informing us that below Cawnpore all was tranquil—daks running and telegraph communication with Calcutta open, just as before the mutiny, and that Lucknow was quite safe; so much so that the army was to move on Futtehghur before making any fresh attempt for its relief. The messenger, however, strongly urged us not to attempt to escape down the Ganges, as we should certainly be seized and killed by the rebels along the banks; but to remain quietly where we were until Havelock's army advanced and captured Futtehghur.

Tuesday, 25th.—My messenger, Rohna, arrived to-day from Nynee Tal with a welcome letter from my wife, giving good accounts of herself and Gracey. They, with the other ladies, had been removed as a matter of precaution to Almorah, as Khan Bahadur Khan's troops were threatening Nynee Tal. Rohna brought me also a little note from Ramsay, entreating me not to attempt to reach the hills by Pillibheet, as the country is much disturbed and full of rebels; so that this route is quite impracticable. These letters gave us a good account of affairs generally. Reinforcements had reached Delhi; which, it was hoped, might fall by the end of the month, and twenty thousand men are announced on their way from

England. It appears that communication is open between Nynee Tal, Mussoorie, and other parts, as accounts up to the 18th June have reached my wife of all the dear ones at home, who were quite well, and in happy ignorance of our desperate situation.

Late in the evening, one of Hurdeo Buksh's people came from Dhurumpore to tell us that a messenger, sent by his master to ascertain the state of the river, had returned and reported all clear and safe as far as Cawnpore. As it is now pretty certain that we shall make the attempt ere many days elapse, we deemed it right to intimate our intention to Major Robertson and Mr. Churcher, in order that they might accompany us. Probyn accordingly sent a note to Robertson to warn him, but enjoining him to maintain entire secrecy, as upon this mainly depends our safety and the success of our enterprise.

Wednesday, August 26th.—General Havelock's messenger again advised us strongly against attempting the river route; maintaining that at several points on the banks on both sides, to his certain knowledge, the enemy were posted in force with guns, which of course we could never pass. We sent Wuzeer Singh to tell Hurdeo Buksh what the hurkarah had told us. On his return he said that information to the same effect had also reached Hurdeo Buksh, who had in consequence sent off fresh messengers to procure accurate intelligence, as to the state of the river and the position of the rebels between us and Cawnpore. We are not to start until they return. All this is very depressing: we seem to be surrounded by a circle of fire, which it is impossible to pass through. All that we can do is, like Ezra, with earnest prayer to seek of our God "a right way for us and the little ones."

A messenger arrived to-day bringing a letter from Delhi, which was, as usual, concealed in the sole of his shoe. On opening it, we found to our great disappointment that it was not addressed to either of us; but was from Yule (of the 9th Lancers, we suppose,) to an officer of the name of Beatson at Cawnpore. The messenger said he left Delhi on the 18th, when all was going on well. On the 12th an outwork was carried by our troops without much loss, the enemy losing five hundred killed: they daily sally out and attack our siege operations, but do little mischief, and cause us no loss. Reinforcements from Bombay, the messenger said, had arrived, and a siege train from

Ferozepore was close at hand, which it was hoped would at once settle the business.

Thursday, 27th August.—Nothing new settled about our plans, and we are much harassed. Heavy guns firing in Furruckabad to-day, we know not from what cause; but they reminded us painfully of our fearful proximity to that place where are so many thirsting for our lives. Amidst it all, to-day's Psalms most consoling, and wonderfully suited to our case, especially the 121st.

A Brahmin in the employ of Mr. Churcher, and said to be much in his confidence, came to us to-day bringing a letter from Major Robertson, telling us that although so weak that he faints whenever he is moved in order to have his wound dressed, he thought it his duty to avail himself of this opportunity, which God has put in his way, to try to escape from these awful dangers which threaten us on every side. Although he considers our chance of escape very slender, and the attempt a desperate one, he will hold himself in readiness to start to join our boat whenever he receives instructions of the time fixed for departure. The Brahmin did his best to dissuade us from the attempt; assuring us it must end in our destruction, unless Hurdeo Buksh would send down with us at least four hundred matchlockmen in separate boats. Mr. Churcher, he told us, would certainly not run the risk, but preferred remaining where he was, in hiding with the Aheers. We dismissed the messenger, telling him to inform his master that we are quite determined to start as soon as the boat is ready.

Saturday, 29th August.—Late last night, after we were all in bed, but none of us asleep, and while pondering over our gloomy circumstances, Jones, who has a very fine voice, suddenly commenced singing the "Old Folks at Home." I never felt more deeply affected in my life; and, indeed, this was the case with all of us while listening to the song.

Seetah Ram soon after arrived, bringing a note to me from General Havelock, and another to Hurdeo Buksh's address; both enclosed in quills, and of course very brief. The General strongly recommended us to remain where we were and watch events; as the rebels infested all the roads and rendered travelling most dangerous—almost impossible. We were much cast down, and consulted together whether to follow the General's advice and remain where we were, or risk the river journey. It was, after all, but a choice of dangers: to remain where we were much longer was almost certain destruction; to go, although hazardous in the extreme, offered at least a chance of safety and escape, so we all three determined to try the river. There was no time to lose, as Seetah Ram reported that the rebels were again collecting, but that as yet there were no bodies of men and no guns on the river banks.

We all thought it best that Probyn should go at once to Hurdeo Buksh, deliver to him General Havelock's letter, and intimate that we were ready to start as soon as he pleased. He accordingly set off, and returned in about two hours, stating that Hurdeo Buksh has determined to send us off by boat to-morrow morning. May God in his infinite mercy go forth with us, and protect us, and bring us to our desired haven! We sent off a messenger to Robertson to inform him and Churcher, and also bearers to convey the former, as he could not walk to the boat to-morrow morning.

Tuesday, September 1st.—On Sunday, August 30th, I awoke very early, and roused up the others. The morning was dull and rainy, just fit for our expedition. We all in that little shed joined, for the last time, in earnest prayer together for a blessing on our undertaking, and in thanksgiving for the many mercies we had received, and for our wonderful preservation hitherto in this place. At 7 A.M., Hurdeo Buksh came himself to conduct us to the boat. The Thakoors, and other leading men of the village, who had been in the habit of coming and sitting with us and giving us the news during the past weary weeks, accompanied us to the boats; which we found moored on the Ramgunga, opposite Dhurumpore, and all ready for us.

Our party consisted of eleven matchlockmen, as a guard, eight rowers, all under the command of Hurdeo Buksh's brother-in-law Thakoor Pirthee Pal. Seetah Ram also accompanied us, as he knew where our troops were located at Cawnpore, and might be useful to us *en route;* and also Rohna, who was to return at once if we reached Cawnpore in safety, with a note to Hurdeo Buksh, and one for my wife, to take on to Nynee Tal. One of the Kussowrah Thakoors, of Poorun, also went with us.

We remained for more than two hours at the boat, waiting for Major Robertson and Mr. Churcher, and at the imminent peril of our own lives; our safety mainly depending on expedition and secrecy. If intelligence of our projected attempt reached the Nawab and Subahdars in Futtehghur nothing was easier than for them to detach some sepoys down the Ganges, to the point where the Ramgunga falls into it, and intercept us there. They could reach that point in less than two hours with ease from the time of starting; whereas it would occupy nearly from morn till evening, owing to the winding course of the Ramgunga, before we could hope to enter the Ganges.

Hurdeo Buksh had happily taken the precaution, the night before, of seizing all the boats at the ferries on both rivers, within the limits of his domain, thus cutting off all communication with Furruckabad. Any lengthened interruption of the passages across the Ganges would not fail, however, to attract notice and excite suspicion; and it was in his opinion very essential for our safety that we should embark and start without further loss of time. We were in a most painful position. We could not bear the idea of leaving our poor countrymen behind, and yet if we delayed any longer, we might lose our own lives without benefiting them. At last, just as our patience was exhausted, a messenger arrived from Major Robertson to say that neither he nor Mr. Churcher would risk the attempt. They were doubtless dissuaded by the Brahmin servant of Mr. Churcher, who had used his best arguments to deter us from the journey.

There was nothing now to detain us, so about eleven, as far as we could judge, we started. Hurdeo Buksh rode with us for some miles along the banks of the stream and then left us; enjoining us to be careful to remain under the covered part of the boat, and on no account to show ourselves, as that would lead to our discovery, and in such an event to our destruction. To secure the fidelity of the boatmen, he had, he informed us, seized their families, who would only be released on the news reaching him of our safe arrival at Cawnpore. The matchlockmen were his own immediate retainers, and fully trustworthy. I, however, doubted them much more than the boatmen, for whose fidelity, we have a substantial guarantee; for I believed they would take to the river, in which they can swim like fish, on the very first approach of danger.

The boat was nominally conveying the female portion of the family of a relative of Hurdeo Buksh, on a visit to their relations at a lonely place on the Oude side of the Ganges called Tirrowah Pulleeah, belonging to a Talookdar named

Dhunna Singh. This man is a great friend of Hurdeo Buksh, and possessed of considerable influence on both sides of the river, as far as Cawnpore. If he considered the road safe he was to accompany us to that place; if he did not, he was to give us shelter and protect us for the time being, and until something was determined upon for our disposal.

For the first twenty miles of our course down the Ramgunga, we ran little risk, as Hurdeo Buksh's influence sufficed to protect us. For the last thirty, until the river joins the Ganges, the danger was great. Messengers, however, met us at different points along the bank to warn us whether we might safely proceed or not. At one point we were in considerable danger of being wrecked. The boatmen tried a new channel and came upon a rapid, with an abrupt fall of, I should think, nearly four feet. The stream was running with great rapidity; but from its shallowness, the boat stuck in the middle, and for ten minutes could not be extricated. We dared not show ourselves outside, and it was most tying to sit still, crowded as we were in the close covered space allotted to us, while the boat hung as it were on an inclined plane, the water roaring and surging round us. At last they managed to get her clear, and we floated down, without further interruption, till we reached within two or three miles of the mouth of the Ramgunga.

The river had so materially changed its channel this year, that for several reaches, we found ourselves directly opposite the village of Kassim Kore, situated on the right bank of the Ganges, and which we supposed lay some four miles higher up the stream. This village bore the worst character; its inhabitants had, we were aware, taken an active part in the massacre of the Futtehghur fugitives and the plunder of their boat; that fearful tragedy having occurred in its immediate neighbourhood.

It was with breathless anxiety, therefore, that we watched this village. From the great height of the bank on which it was placed the people must have seen us, as we came winding down the stream and rounded the reaches: and the unusual sight of a boat could not, we feared, fail to attract attraction, and lead parties of them to come off in boats to intercept us. The sun was setting as we floated out into the Ganges, here about a mile broad, and only about a quarter of a mile below Kassim Kore. It was with a sickening sort of anxiety we continued to watch this place; but it was like a village of the dead: not a human being could we discern moving about, and deeply thankful did we feel when we found that we were passing unnoticed. But we scarcely ventured to consider ourselves secure, until we lost sight of the hateful spot in the distance.

The Ganges was still in flood, and we floated down very rapidly, keeping, as far as it was possible, the middle of the stream. At one point where the stream narrowed considerably, there was a ferry close to a large village, with several boats close to the bank, and a number of people collected and about to cross. Except the boat at these and other ferries, there was nothing floating on the Ganges. Instead of the fleets which for the last fifty years had been passing up and down without intermission, not a single boat had been seen on its waters since that one which had escaped from Futtehghur, and of whose fate we were in the utmost ignorance. The unusual sight of a boat rowed rapidly down stream, with a number of armed men on the roof and deck, attracted immediate attention, and we hardly dared to hope that we could safely pass this ferry. As we approached the place, our guards got their cartridge boxes handy, and their powder horns by them, all ready, if required.

We were, as we expected, challenged and asked who we were, and told to stop and pull in shore. The Thakoor replied that he was taking his family down to Tirhowah Pulleeah, and could not stop. A voice called out, "You have Feringees (English) concealed in that boat; come ashore at once." "Feringees on board," was the ready answer of the Thakoor, Pirthee Pal, "I wish we had, and we should soon dispose of them and get their plunder."—"Stop and come ashore," was repeated; but by this time, owing to the rapidity of the stream, we had floated past.

The river widened, and we bore out into the centre of the stream; the distance thus put between us, and the sight of the guard all ready with their matchlocks, no doubt deterred any of those on shore from putting off and following us. After this we passed on without challenge until nightfall, when the boat was stopped; we anchored at a most solitary, desolate place covered with long grass, and left half-dry by the receding waters of the river. This place, we heard, was only a mile and a half from Tirrowah Pulleeah, Dhunna Singh's stronghold. Our crew and guards immediately went on shore, and commenced cooking.

It was, of course, essential for us to communicate with Dhunna Singh, as he was to accompany us on, and it would be hopeless for us to attempt to proceed without him. Only one of our party, a boatman, knew the way to his Fort, which lay directly across the waste, alongside of which we were anchored: with, as he told us, a deep creek intervening, and he declared he would not go alone at this time of night. Some of the guard and boatmen were in vain ordered to accompany this man; not one would leave his cooking. At last the Thakoors seized one of the boatmen, gave him a sound thrashing, and frightened him into accompanying them.

They followed a small path, and were soon lost in the long grass. Probyn and I got out of the boat and walked up and down the bank, anxiously discussing the probability of the messengers failing us, or in event even of their reaching the place, of Dhunna Singh's answering our summons or not. It was the wildest and most dismal scene I have ever witnessed; the boatmen and guard even seemed depressed, and sat cooking in silence: not a sound was heard, but the croaking of innumerable frogs in the pools, and crabs in the swamp. Nearly two hours passed away without any sign of our messengers: not a soul came near us. At last Probyn determined that we had better go on at all hazards, as the night was slipping away; and as the most dangerous part of the river was before us, it was necessary to pass it under cover of the darkness. Desolate as the place was, it would not do to remain there for the night; as the herdsmen grazing their cattle would no doubt discover us as soon as it was light, and most likely give information to the villagers, who would come down and destroy us. My opinion was strongly against starting without Dhunna Singh. It had been part of Hurdeo Buksh's arrangement that he should accompany us, and if once we deviated from it, in so important a point, the crew might not consider themselves any longer responsible for our safety, and might desert us. Probyn agreed to remain for another half-hour: one of terrible anxiety and suspense it was.

I was pacing up and down, and almost in despair, when I heard the sound of voices approaching, and Dhunna Singh almost immediately came up with our messengers and a few followers; he was an old man with a white head, but very wiry and athletic, and from his frank and self-possessed manner, I saw at once that he was the right sort of man for this kind of work. He said we must go on at once; and lamented that so much time had already been lost, as it was most desirable to be beyond a part of the river near Sheorajpore by the morning. The only thing suspicious about Dhunna Singh was his desiring to accompany us in a small boat to be towed astern, instead of on board ours. I told him we expected him to come into our boat; and this he did, after some hesitation.

We started about ten o'clock, so far as we could judge, and floated rapidly down the river, keeping as much as we could in the centre of the stream. We were challenged repeatedly from either bank and ordered to stop and come ashore; but on starting, Dhunna Singh had instructed two of his men, whom he had brought on board with him, to reply in answer to any challenge, that the boat belonged to Dhunna Singh of Tirowah Pulleeah, who was taking his family down to bathe at a celebrated bathing ghaut near Cawnpore. If this explanation failed to satisfy, the men in repeating it were instructed to say that Dhunna Singh was himself on board; and if even this did not suffice, he would himself come forward and answer the challenge.

On several occasions he had to do this; for the explanation of the men being not believed, a second and more peremptory summons was given to stop and pull ashore. Dhunna Singh's own powerful and peculiarly harsh voice, however, never failed to satisfy inquirers; who, on hearing his explanation, either remained silent, or said, "Go on, go on!" At one village, however, much embarrassment was caused by the party challenging being intimate with Dhunna Singh, expressing great satisfaction at his arrival, and begging him to come ashore and take them on board. Dhunna Singh showed great readiness and presence of mind in this difficulty. He answered their hail with great apparent cordiality, and telling the rowers to stop pulling, began asking questions about different persons and places; he thus held the party in conversation till we had floated well past the village, when he called out that he could not stop just then, as he wanted his family to be at the ghaut in time to bathe before the morning; but that on his return, in two or three days, he would make a point of stopping in the village. On saying this, he ordered the men to give way as fast as possible, which they did; and as the river was running like a sluice, we passed down so rapidly, that any attempt to have pursued us by a boat from the village would have been quite vain.

About one in the morning, we approached Mendee Ghaut, the chief ferry between Oude and the Futtehghur side of the river, and a great place of resort for mutineers or rebels. Dhunna Sing expressed great anxiety to pass this place in safety; assuring us that the risk of detection was very great. Most providentially, as we approached within a mile of the place, a large bank of clouds came over the moon and it became partially dark. The rowers were told to ship their oars, and the whole party to keep profound silence. In this way we glided down the stream very rapidly, and silent as the grave; owing to the darkness and perfect stillness we passed this critical point altogether unnoticed and unchallenged. About an hour after this we grounded twice: the first time, the boat was got off without much trouble; but on the second occasion she struck several times very heavily, and then nearly capsized. She, however, soon righted a little, but remained for more than an hour stuck fast on the sand-bank. I thought then it surely was all up with us; that we could not float her, and that we should be deserted by those on board and left to the mercy of the villagers, who could not fail to notice and come down on us as soon as it was light.

Nearly the whole of the guard, as well as the rowers, at our earnest entreaty, got into the water, and, by thus lightening the boat, succeeded, after heavy labour, in getting her afloat. The delay caused by this mishap was very serious; for day broke just as we were nearing a place on the right bank where a body of the enemy with guns were said to be posted, and which we had calculated upon passing during the night.

As we approached this point, Dhunna Singh, as well as ourselves, felt most anxious. Great, however, was our relief, and deep our thankfulness, when, upon rounding a reach of the river, we found this place silent and deserted. Had the enemy been here we must have fallen into their hands; for escape would have been impossible. Dhunna Singh now told us that if we could only succeed in reaching Bithoor, some ten miles further down, which he supposed was occupied by our troops, we should be safe; but until we arrived there, as it was now daylight, the risk of being stopped was great.

On we went without interruption for some miles, when the stream carrying us close in shore on the right bank, we came, on rounding a point suddenly, on a considerable body of people, some bathing and some sitting on the bank. On Dhunna Singh replying in the usual manner to their challenge, what was our delight and surprise to hear the party, who were completely deceived about us, earnestly warn Dhunna Singh not to proceed much further down the river, as he would in that case inevitably fall into the hands of the Gora log, (Europeans) who were in force in Bithoor, and would kill all in the boat.

Dhunna Singh, with his usual presence of mind, affected great alarm at this intelligence, and winking coolly at me as I lay inside the covering, eagerly inquired of those ashore where our troops were posted, and how far we could proceed down the stream with saftety. He was told the exact spot, and then, saying he would avoid that point, and cross to the Oude side of the stream, told the rowers to give way. We shot rapidly away, and thus escaped a most imminent danger. So near were we to the party on shore, that Probyn and I each caught up one of the children and kept our hands on their mouths, lest they might speak or cry out; which would have betrayed us at once, and we must have been lost.

We met with no incident for the next few miles, and about 11 o'clock we reached Bithoor. We were now beginning to congratulate ourselves that at last we were in safety, and Dhunna Singh, as we approached the place, removed the curtain hanging in front of where we lay, and called out to us, "You are now in your own territory; come out and look about, for there is no more need of hiding." Jones was just on the point of availing himself of this permission, and going out from under cover (where he had been cramped up all night), into the open air, when, as he was stepping over me I caught his leg, and by some involuntary impulse begged of him to stop, and not show himself for a little. He had scarcely done so, and the words had hardly left my lips, when the curtain was hastily replaced, and we were hailed by a man on the bank. Dhunna Singh inquired who he was;

he replied that he was a sepoy of Jussa Singh's son, and had come across from Futtehpore Chowrassee with some of the Nana's people, to convey away some of the Nana's property, which he had been forced to leave behind him when he fled from our troops on their capture of the place.

Dhunna Singh completely deceived this man by his ready replies to all his questions, and so prevented his suspecting the real character of the boat, or giving the alarm. Dhunna Singh expressed great satisfaction on hearing that Bithoor was evacuated by our troops, and reoccupied by some of the Nana's, and of his ally Jussa Singh's son. Jussa Singh himself, who was the Nana's confederate in the Cawnpore tragedy, had about a fortnight previously died of his wounds, and been succeeded by his son; with whom the Nana was at this moment in hiding a few miles from us, at Futtehpore Chowrassee.

Soon after passing this sepoy, and while floating past some high buildings, several shots were fired in rapid succession; and we saw several hundred armed men congregated in and around the buildings. We, however, heard no whiz of bullets, and supposed that the firing was in honour of the great Mahomedan festival of the

Mohurrum, which is now being celebrated. It was truly miraculous how we escaped being observed by this large body of men, all armed, and in the service of our deadliest enemies. We were the sole boat which had appeared for nearly two months on the river, and the unusual sight could not fail to have drawn their attention to us, and yet no one molested us, or tried to stop us.

An hour of most intense anxiety passed in getting clear of this dreadful place, Bithoor. When we had left it about two miles behind, Dhunna Singh, who as well as myself had not closed an eye all night, came in and lay down under the cover of the boat, and, assuring us that we were now all right, said he could take a sleep. Soon after we had the great joy of seeing Cawnpore in the distance.

Owing to the frequent turns of the river, and a high contrary wind which had sprung up, we were a weary long time in approaching the station.

Just as our hopes of safety appeared on the verge of accomplishment, they suddenly seemed about to be entirely defeated; for the wind caught our boat, and in spite of the efforts of the rowers, who were by this time thoroughly worn out, drove us half-across to the Oude side of the river. We then, for the first time, became aware that this bank was occupied by a body of the enemy watching the Cawnpore force. Their tents became distinctly visible; and, as we were being driven across, we heard their drums and bugles sounding the alarm; as they, I fancy, took us for a reconnoitring party. We expected that they would fire at us; but fortunately they did not, and the wind falling we were enabled, after much labour, to get back again to our own side.

Soon after we came upon a picket of Sikhs posted near the old Magazine. This was the most joyful sight our eyes had seen for many a weary day and night. The party, not imagining that by any possibility the boat could contain friends, came down to oppose us, and were capping their muskets to fire, when Wuzeer Singh hailed them in. their own dialect, informing them who we were. The native officer in command, and all the men, then came forward to congratulate us on our escape; at which they seemed as heartily rejoiced as if they had been our own countrymen. They told us to drop down the stream until we came to the camp where our troops were entrenched, which we should know by a steamer being moored below. We left them, and in about half an hour reached the landing. After some trouble, owing to the violence of the wind and strength of the current, we succeeded in making our boat fast to another alongside the steamer. Then, indeed, with grateful and overflowing hearts, we stepped on shore, feeling that at last we were saved, and among our own countrymen.

We landed about two P.M. of the 31st August, just twenty-seven hours after we started; during which time we had run the gauntlet for more than 150 miles of river way, through the midst of the enemy's country. A picket of her Majesty's 84th Regiment was on duty at the ghaut. The men congregated round us, and even our own flesh and blood could not have more repeatedly or warmly congratulated us on our safety than they did: they were very tender of poor Mrs. Probyn, and insisted on carrying the children and our little baggage to wherever we wished to go. On learning that the magistrate's tent was a few yards off at the top of the bank, I immediately went there, and found Sherer of our service. On announcing myself (for being in native dress he could not recognise me) he was as much surprised as if he had seen an apparition;

for I had long been reported among the killed at Futtehghur. I can never forget his hearty welcome.

I was just able to tell him that the Probyns and their children were down at the boat and beg of him to go and bring them, when, as he rushed off for that purpose, everything seemed to swim around me, and I fell on the ground from excitement and exhaustion. Sherer soon after returned with the Probyns and by that time I had recovered myself. When we had all collected in the tent, our first question was as to the fate of the party who had left Futtehghur, and of whom we hoped that some had escaped. Then for the first time we heard the truth, that they had really *all* been murdered: that not one had survived. We also heard of the awful massacre at Cawnpore, of which only vague rumours had hitherto reached us, too terrible to admit of credence. We could scarcely believe that we four persons and the two children are the sole survivors of that large body of our country-people, men, women, and children.

Sherer got rooms prepared for us in a house fitted up as an hotel, close to his tents, and just beyond the entrenchment occupied by our troops.

To get to this place we were obliged to pass the house in which the slaughter had been perpetrated, and the well where so many of those dear friends lie, whom we had so lately parted with in full strength and vigour.

When we found ourselves in a house again, for the first time for three months, and in a position of comparative security, we felt quite awe-struck; and, with hearts overflowing with thankfulness, we knelt down together to bless our God who had so wonderfully "delivered us from the hand of the enemy, and from those who lay in wait for us by the way."

THE END.

NEW WORKS ON INDIAN AFFAIRS.

1.

PERSONAL ADVENTURES DURING THE INDIAN REBELLION IN ROHILCUND, FUTTEHGHUR, AND OUDE. By W. Edwards, Esq., B.C.S., Judge of Benares, and late Magistrate and Collector of Budaon, in Rohilcund. 3rd Edition, Post 8vo. Price 6*s.* cloth.

"For touching incidents, hair-breadth 'scapes, and the pathos of sufferings almost incredible, there has appeared nothing like this little book of personal adventures. . . . . We have here a tale of suffering which may have been equalled, but never surpassed. Surely if fictitious stories of affliction, coined from the imagination, have been sold by countless thousands, these real adventures, which no effort of the imagination can surpass, will find a sympathising public."—*Athenæum.*

"Mr. Edwards' narrative is one of the most deeply interesting episodes of a story of which the least striking portions cannot be read without emotion. He tells his story with simplicity and manliness, and it bears the impress of that earnest and unaffected reference to the hand and will of God which was the stay and comfort of many other of those brave hearts who bore so well the tremendous test to which they were in a moment called to submit themselves."—*Guardian.*

"Among the stories of hair-breadth escapes which have arisen out of the sudden and great peril into which our countrymen in India were cast by the outbreak of the revolt, this is one of the most interesting and touching."—*Examiner.*

"Mr. Edwards has compiled a very touching narrative of his wanderings and adventures."—*Literary Gazette.*

"A simple and deeply interesting account of three months personal adventures among the natives of Rohilcund and Oude."—*Economist.*

"So great is the unity of the interest that no account of it can do it justice."—*Globe.*

2.

EIGHT MONTHS' CAMPAIGN AGAINST THE BENGAL SEPOYS, DURING THE MUTINY, 1857. By George Bourchier, Captain Bengal Horse Artillery. With Plans. Post 8vo. Price 7*s.* 6*d.* cloth.

"Colonel Bourchier has given a right manly, fair, and forcible statement of events, and the reader will derive much pleasure and instruction from his pages."—*Athenæum.*

"We can fairly recommend Colonel Bourchier's narrative as a succinct and readable history of those operations in which he personally took part, during his campaign of eight months against the mutineers of Bengal."—*Economist.*

"The narrative is clear and lucid, and intensely exciting; but it possesses an infinitely greater value, inasmuch as it exhibits throughout a manly, kind, and patriotic spirit."—*Daily Telegraph.*

"None who really desire to be more than very superficially acquainted with the rise and progress of the rebellion may consider their studies complete until they have read Colonel Bourchier. The nicely engraved plans from the colonel's own sketches, confer additional value upon his contribution to the literature of the Indian war."—*Leader.*

"Colonel Bourchier relates his adventures in a free and graceful manner, never giving an undue prominence to his own actions, and never withholding praise from the gallant deeds of others."—*Critic.*

"This is a valuable addition to the works already published on the Indian revolt."—*Ladies' Newspaper.*

3.

THE CHAPLAIN'S NARRATIVE OF THE SIEGE OF DELHI. By the Rev. J. E. W. ROTTON, Chaplain to the Forces. Post 8vo. With a Plan of the City and Siege Works. Price 10*s*. 6*d*., cloth.

"A simple and touching statement which bears the impress of truth in every word."—*Athenæum*.

"A plain unvarnished record of what came under a field chaplain's daily observation. Our author is a sincere, hard-working, and generous-minded man."—*Leader*.

"An earnest record by a Christian minister of some of the most touching scenes that can come under observation."—*Literary Gazette*.

"The Chaplain's Narrative is remarkable for its pictures of men in a moral and religious aspect during the progress of a harassing siege, when suddenly stricken down by the enemy or disease."—*Spectator*.

4.

THE CRISIS IN THE PUNJAB, from the 10th of May until the Fall of Delhi. By FREDERICK COOPER, Esq., C.S., Umritsur. Post 8vo. Price 7*s*. 6*d*., cloth.

"From Mr. Cooper's narrative we are enabled to appreciate the wonderful energy, foresight, and determination of Sir John Lawrence and the other authorities at Lahore, by which alone a dreadful catastrophe was arrested in the Punjab, Delhi reconquered, and Agra preserved."—*Athenæum*.

"The narrative is written with vigour and earnestness, and is full of the most terrible and tragic interest."—*Economist*.

"What the 'Crisis in the Punjab' thoroughly does, is to give an account of the mutinous outbreaks at the different stations and the manner in which they were met. . . . . A considerable part of it is fresh and graphic, especially in the description of the military proceedings to effect the disarming."—*Spectator*.

"One of the most interesting and spirited books which have sprung out of the sepoy mutiny."—*Globe*.

5.

THE DEFENCE OF LUCKNOW: A Diary recording the Daily Events of the Siege from 31st May to 25th September, 1857. By Captain THOMAS F. WILSON, 13th Bengal N.I., Assistant-Adjutant-General. 6th Thousand. Small post 8vo, price 2*s*. 6*d*., with Plan of Residency.

"The characteristics of this book are clear arrangement and impressive accuracy." —*Quarterly Review*.

"It deserves to pass from hand to hand, and not to be laid down until the last line has been read."—*Leader*.

"The Staff-Officer supplies exact military information with brevity and distinctness."—*Globe*.

"We commend the Staff-Officer's Diary to the attention of our readers for its unostentatious relation of facts, recorded with a degree of distinction that vouches for the authenticity of the writer's statements."—*Press*.

"The story of the glorious garrison of Lucknow is told in this volume with all its thrilling details."—*Nonconformist*.

LONDON: SMITH, ELDER AND CO., 65, CORNHILL.

65, *Cornhill, London, September*, 1858.

NEW AND STANDARD WORKS

PUBLISHED BY

SMITH, ELDER & Co.

WORKS IN THE PRESS.

Social Innovators and their Schemes. By WILLIAM LUCAS SARGANT, Author of "The Science of Social Opulence," &c.

Post 8vo.

Indian Scenes and Characters, Sketched from Life. By Prince ALEXIS SOLTYKOFF.

Sixteen Plates in Tinted Lithography, with Descriptions. Colombier Folio. *(Nearly Ready.)*

Christianity in India. By JOHN WILLIAM KAYE, Author of "Life of Lord Metcalfe," &c.

8vo. *(In the Press.)*

Lectures and Addresses on Literary and Social Topics. By the late Rev. FRED. W. ROBERTSON, of Brighton. *Post 8vo.* *(Just Ready.)*

Tents and Tent Life. By Capt. GODFREY RHODES, 94th Regt. *Post 8vo, with Twenty-eight Plates, 12s. cloth.*

The Life of J. Deacon Hume, Esq., late Secretary to the Board of Trade. By the Rev. CHARLES BADHAM. *Post 8vo.*

Phantastes: a Faerie Romance for Men and Women. By GEORGE MACDONALD, Author of "Within and Without." *Post 8vo.*

Historic Notes on the Old and New Testament. By SAMUEL SHARPE, Esq.

New and Revised Edition. Post 8vo.

The Parents' Cabinet of Amusement and Instruction, for Young Persons.

A New and Revised Edition.

In Shilling Volumes, Post 8vo, with a Frontispiece printed in Oil Colours, and numerous Woodcuts, in a handsome Illustrated Binding.

VOLUME I. WILL BE PUBLISHED ON THE 1ST OF DECEMBER.

NEW PUBLICATIONS.

CHEAPER EDITION.

The Life of Charlotte Brontë. (CURRER BELL.) Author of "JANE EYRE," "SHIRLEY," "VILLETTE," &c. By MRS. GASKELL, Author of "North and South," &c.

Fourth Edition, Revised, One Volume, with a Portrait of Miss Brontë and a View of Haworth Parsonage. Price 7s. 6d.

"All the secrets of the literary workmanship of the authoress of 'Jane Eyre' are unfolded in the course of this extraordinary narrative."—*Times.*

"Mrs. Gaskell has produced one of the best biographies of a woman by a woman which we can recall to mind."—*Athenæum.*

Gunnery in 1858: *being a Treatise on Rifles, Cannon, and Sporting Arms.* By WILLIAM GREENER, Author of "The Gun."

Demy 8vo, with Illustrations, price 14s., cloth.

Personal Adventures during the Indian Rebellion, in Rohilcund, Futteghur, and Oude. By W. EDWARDS, Esq., B.C.S.

Post 8vo, price 6s. cloth.

"For touching incidents, hair-breadth 'scapes, and the pathos of sufferings almost incredible, there has appeared nothing like this little book of 'Personal Adventures.'"—*Athenæum.*

"Among the stories of hair-breadth escapes in India this is one of the most interesting and touching."—*Examiner.*

"A very touching narrative."—*Lit. Gazette.*

"No account of it can do it justice."—*Globe.*

The Crisis in the Punjab. By FREDERICK H. COOPER, Esq., C.S., Umritsir.

Post 8vo, with Map, price 7s. 6d. cloth.

"The book is full of terrible interest. The narrative is written with vigour and earnestness, and is full of the most tragic interest."—*Economist.*

"One of the most interesting and spirited books which have sprung out of the sepoy mutiny."—*Globe.*

Eight Months' Campaign against the Bengal Sepoys, during the Mutiny, 1857. By Colonel GEORGE BOURCHIER, C.B., Bengal Horse Artillery.

With Plans. Post 8vo, price 7s. 6d. cloth.

"A right manly, fair, and forcible statement of events."—*Athenæum.*

"Colonel Bouchier relates his adventures in a free and graceful manner."—*Literary Gazette.*

The Parsees: their History, Religion, Manners, and Customs. By DOSABHOY FRAMJEE.

Post 8vo, price 10s. cloth.

"An acceptable addition to our literature. It gives information which many will be glad to have carefully gathered together, and formed into a shapely whole."—*Economist.*

Homely Ballads for the Working Man's Fireside. By MARY SEWELL.

Post 8vo, cloth, One Shilling.

MR. RUSKIN'S WORKS ON ART.

Notes on the Pictures in the Exhibition of the Royal Academy, &c., for 1858. By JOHN RUSKIN.

Fifth Thousand. 8*vo, price One Shilling.*

The Political Economy of Art. *Price* 2*s.* 6*d. cloth.*

"A most able, eloquent, and well-timed work. We hail it with satisfaction, thinking it calculated to do much practical good, and we cordially recommend it to our readers."—*Witness.*

"Mr. Ruskin's chief purpose is to treat the artist's power, and the art itself, as items of the world's wealth, and to show how these may be best evolved, produced, accumulated, and distributed."—*Athenæum.*

"We never quit Mr. Ruskin without being the better for what he has told us, and we therefore recommend this little volume, like all his other works, to the perusal of our readers." —*Economist.*

"This book, daring, as it is, glances keenly at principles, of which some are among the articles of ancient codes, while others are evolving slowly to the light."—*Leader.*

The Elements of Drawing.

Second Edition. Crown 8*vo. With Illustrations drawn by the Author. Price* 7*s.* 6*d., cloth.*

"The rules are clearly and fully laid down; and the earlier exercises always conducive to the end by simple and unembarrassing means. The whole volume is full of liveliness."—*Spectator.*

"We close this book with a feeling that, though nothing supersedes a master, yet that no student of art should launch forth without this work as a compass."—*Athenæum.*

"It will be found not only an invaluable acquisition to the student, but agreeable and instructive reading for any one who wishes to refine his perceptions of natural scenery, and of its worthiest artistic representations."—*Economist.*

"Original as this treatise is, it cannot fail to be at once instructive and suggestive."—*Literary Gazette.*

"The most useful and practical book on the subject which has ever come under our notice."—*Press.*

Modern Painters, Vol. IV. On Mountain Beauty.

Imperial 8*vo, with Thirty-five Illustrations engraved on Steel, and* 116 *Woodcuts, drawn by the Author. Price* 2*l.* 10*s. cloth.*

"Considered as an illustrated volume, this is the most remarkable which Mr. Ruskin has yet issued. The plates and woodcuts are profuse, and include numerous drawings of mountain form by the author, which prove Mr. Ruskin to be essentially an artist. He is an unique man, both among artists and writers."—*Spectator.*

"The present volume of Mr. Ruskin's elaborate work treats chiefly of mountain scenery, and discusses at length the principles involved in the pleasure we derive from mountains and their pictorial representation. The singular beauty of his style, the hearty sympathy with all forms of natural loveliness, the profusion of his illustrations form irresistible attractions."—*Daily News.*

Modern Painters, Vol. III. Of Many Things.

With Eighteen Illustrations drawn by the Author, and engraved on Steel. Price 38*s. cloth.*

"Every one who cares about nature, or poetry, or the story of human development —every one who has a tinge of literature or philosophy, will find something that is for him in this volume."—*Westminster Review.*

"Mr. Ruskin is in possession of a clear and penetrating mind; he is undeniably practical in his fundamental ideas; full of the deepest reverence for all that appears to him beautiful and holy. His style is, as usual, clear, bold, racy. Mr. Ruskin is one of the first writers of the day."—*Economist.*

"The present volume, viewed as a literary achievement, is the highest and most striking evidence of the author's abilities that has yet been published."—*Leader.*

"All, it is to be hoped, will read the book for themselves. They will find it well worth a careful perusal."—*Saturday Review.*

WORKS OF MR. RUSKIN—*continued.*

Modern Painters. Vols. I. and II.

Imp. 8vo. Vol. I., 5th Edit., 18s. cloth. Vol. II., 4th Edit., 10s. 6d. cloth.

"Mr. Ruskin's work will send the painter more than ever to the study of nature; will train men who have always been delighted spectators of nature, to be also attentive observers. Our critics will learn to admire, and mere admirers will learn how to criticise: thus a public will be educated."—*Blackwood's Magazine.*

"A generous and impassioned review of the works of living painters. A hearty and earnest work, full of deep thought, and developing great and striking truths in art."—*British Quarterly Review.*

"A very extraordinary and delightful book, full of truth and goodness, of power and beauty."—*North British Review.*

The Stones of Venice.

Complete in Three Volumes, Imperial 8vo, with Fifty-three Plates and numerous Woodcuts, drawn by the Author. Price 5l. 15s. 6d., cloth.

EACH VOLUME MAY BE HAD SEPARATELY.

Vol. I. THE FOUNDATIONS, *with 21 Plates, price 2l. 2s. 2nd Ed.*
Vol. II. THE SEA STORIES, *with 20 Plates, price 2l. 2s.*
Vol. III. THE FALL, *with 12 Plates, price 1l. 11s. 6d.*

"This book is one which, perhaps, no other man could have written, and one for which the world ought to be and will be thankful. It is in the highest degree eloquent, acute, stimulating to thought, and fertile in suggestion. It will, we are convinced, elevate taste and intellect, raise the tone of moral feeling, kindle benevolence towards men, and increase the love and fear of God."—*Times.*

"The 'Stones of Venice' is the production of an earnest, religious, progressive, and informed mind. The author of this essay on architecture has condensed into it a poetic apprehension, the fruit of awe of God, and delight in nature; a knowledge, love, and just estimate of art; a holding fast to fact and repudiation of hearsay; an historic breadth, and a fearless challenge of existing social problems, whose union we know not where to find paralleled."—*Spectator.*

The Seven Lamps of Architecture.

Second Edition, with Fourteen Plates drawn by the Author. Imperial 8vo. Price 1l. 1s. cloth.

"By the 'Seven Lamps of Architecture,' we understand Mr. Ruskin to mean the seven fundamental and cardinal laws, the observance of and obedience to which are indispensable to the architect, who would deserve the name. The politician, the moralist, the divine, will find in it ample store of instructive matter, as well as the artist. The author of this work belongs to a class of thinkers of whom we have too few amongst us."—*Examiner.*

"Mr. Ruskin's book bears so unmistakeably the marks of keen and accurate observation, of a true and subtle judgment and refined sense of beauty, joined with so much earnestness, so noble a sense of the purposes and business of art, and such a command of rich and glowing language, that it cannot but tell powerfully in producing a more religious view of the uses of architecture, and a deeper insight into its artistic principles."—*Guardian.*

Lectures on Architecture and Painting.

With Fourteen Cuts, drawn by the Author. Second Edition. Crown 8vo. Price 8s. 6d. cloth.

"Mr. Ruskin's lectures—eloquent, graphic, and impassioned—exposing and ridiculing some of the vices of our present system of building, and exciting his hearers by strong motives of duty and pleasure to attend to architecture—are very successful."—*Economist.*

"We conceive it to be impossible that any intelligent persons could listen to the lectures, however they might differ from the judgments asserted, and from the general propositions laid down, without an elevating influence and an aroused enthusiasm."—*Spectator.*

A Portrait of John Ruskin, Esq., Engraved by F. Holl, *from a Drawing by* George Richmond.

Prints, One Guinea; India Proofs, Two Guineas.

RECENT WORKS.

Sermons. By the late REV. FRED. W. ROBERTSON, A.M., Incumbent of Trinity Chapel, Brighton.

FIRST SERIES—*Fourth Edition, Post 8vo, price 9s. cloth.*

SECOND SERIES—*Fourth Edition, price 9s. cloth.*

THIRD SERIES—*Second Edition, Post 8vo, with Portrait, price 9s. cloth.*

"Very beautiful in feeling and occasionally striking and forcible in conception to a remarkable degree."—*Guardian.*

"Mr. Robertson, of Brighton, is a name familiar to most of us, and honoured by all to whom it is familiar."—*Globe.*

"These sermons are full of thought and beauty. There is not a sermon in the series that does not furnish evidence of originality without extravagance, of discrimination without tediousness, and of piety without cant or conventionalism."—*British Quarterly.*

Esmond. By W. M. THACKERAY, ESQ.

A New Edition in One Volume, Crown 8vo, price 6s. cloth.

"Mr. Thackeray has selected for his hero a very noble type of the cavalier softening into the man of the eighteenth century, and for his heroine one of the sweetest women that ever breathed from canvas or from book since Raffaelle painted and Shakspeare wrote."—*Spectator.*

"Apart from its special merits "Esmond" must be read just now as an introduction to "The Virginians." It is quite impossible fully to understand and enjoy the latter story without a knowledge of "Esmond." The new tale is in the strictest sense the sequel of the old, not only introducing the same characters, but continuing their history at a later period."—*Leader.*

Captivity of Russian Princesses in the Caucasus: including a Seven Months' Residence in Shamil's Seraglio, in the Years 1854-5. Translated from the Russian, by H. S. EDWARDS.

With an authentic Portrait of Shamil, a Plan of his House, and a Map. Post 8vo, price 10s. 6d. cloth.

"A book than which there are few novels more interesting. It is a romance of the Caucasus. The account of life in the house of Shamil is full and very entertaining; and of Shamil himself we see much."—*Examiner.*

"The story is certainly one of the most curious we have read; it contains the best popular notice of the social polity of Shamil and the manners of his people."—*Leader.*

"The narrative is well worth reading."—*Athenæum.*

Religion in Common Life. By WILLIAM ELLIS.

Post 8vo, price 7s. 6d. cloth.

"A book addressed to young people of the upper ten thousand upon social duties."—*Examiner.*

"Lessons in Political Economy for young people by a skilful hand."—*Economist.*

The Sea Officer's Manual; being a Compendium of the Duties of a Commander; First, Second, Third, and Fourth Officer; Officer of the Watch; and Midshipman in the Mercantile Navy. By CAPTAIN A. PARISH, of the East India Merchant Service.

Second Edition, Small Post 8vo, price 5s. cloth.

"A very lucid and compendious manual. We would recommend youths intent upon a seafaring life to study it."—*Athenæum.*

"A little book that ought to be in great request among young seamen."—*Examiner.*

RECENT WORKS—*continued.*

Annals of British Legislation, a Classified *Summary of Parliamentary Papers.* Edited by PROFESSOR LEONE LEVI.

THE TWENTY-FIFTH PART IS JUST ISSUED.

Antiquities of Kertch, and Researches in the *Cimmerian Bosphorus.* By DUNCAN MCPHERSON, M.D.,

Imperial Quarto, with Fourteen Plates and numerous Illustrations, including Eight Coloured Fac-Similes of Relics of Antique Art, price Two Guineas.

The Principles of Agriculture; especially *Tropical.* By P. LOVELL PHILLIPS, M.D.

Demy 8vo, price 7s. 6d. cloth.

Westgarth's Victoria, and the Australian Gold *Mines in 1857.*

Post 8vo, with Maps, price 10s. 6d., cloth.

Tauler's Life and Sermons.

Translated by MISS SUSANNA WINKWORTH. With a Preface by the REV. CHARLES KINGSLEY.

Small 4to, Printed on Tinted Paper, and bound in antique style, with red edges, suitable for a Present. Price 15s.

Chandler's Visit to Salt Lake; being a Journey *Across the Plains to the Mormon Settlements at Utah.*

Post 8vo, with a Map, price 9s. cloth.

Doubleday's Life of Sir Robert Peel.

Two Volumes, 8vo, price 18s. cloth.

Cayley's European Revolutions of 1848.

Crown 8vo, price 6s. cloth.

Bunsen's (Chevalier) Signs of the Times; or, *The Dangers to Religious Liberty in the Present Day.* Translated by Miss SUSANNA WINKWORTH.

One Volume, 8vo, price 16s. cloth.

Payn's Stories and Sketches.

Post 8vo, price 8s. 6d. cloth.

Stoney's Residence in Tasmania.

Demy 8vo, with Plates, Cuts, and a Map, price 14s. cloth.

The Court of Henry VIII.: being a Selection *of the Despatches of* SEBASTIAN GIUSTINIAN, *Venetian Ambassador,* 1515-1519. Translated by RAWDON BROWN. *Two Vols., crown 8vo, price 21s. cloth.*

RECENT WORKS—*continued.*

Forbes' (Sir John) Sight-seeing in Germany and the Tyrol.
Post 8vo, with Map and View, price 10s. 6d. cloth.

Undine. From the German of "De la Motte Fouqué."
Price 1s. 6d.

Conolly on the Treatment of the Insane.
Demy 8vo, price 14s. cloth.

Hopkins's Handbook of Average.
8vo, price 12s. 6d. cloth.

Morice's Hand-Book of British Maritime Law.
8vo, price 5s., cloth.

Adams's History and Topography of the Isle of Wight.
Quarto, 25 Steel Plates, cloth, gilt edges, price 2l. 2s.

Waring's Manual of Therapeutics.
Fcap. 8vo, price 12s. 6d. cloth.

Vogel on Disorders of the Blood.
Translated by CHUNDER COOMAR DEY.
8vo, price 7s. 6d. cloth.

Duncan's Campaign with the Turks in Asia.
Two Vols., post 8vo, price 21s. cloth.

Ross's Account of Red River Settlement.
One Volume, post 8vo, price 10s. 6d. cloth.

Ross's Fur Hunters of the Far West.
Two Volumes, post 8vo. With Map and Plate. 21s. cloth.

***Russo-Turkish Campaigns of* 1828-9.**
By COLONEL CHESNEY, R.A., D.C.L., F.R.S.
Third Edition. Post 8vo, with Maps, price 12s. cloth.

Thomson's Military Forces and Institutions of Great Britain. *8vo, price 15s. cloth.*

The Militiaman at Home and Abroad.
With Two Etchings, by JOHN LEECH. *Post 8vo, price 9s. cloth.*

Levi's Manual of the Mercantile Law of Great Britain and Ireland. *8vo, price 12s. cloth.*

Thomson's Laws of War Affecting Commerce and Shipping.
Second Edition, greatly enlarged. 8vo, price 4s. 6d. boards.

WORKS ON INDIA AND THE EAST.

Suggestions Towards the Future Government of India. By Harriet Martineau.

Second Edition. Demy 8*vo, price* 5*s. cloth.*

"The genuine, honest utterances of a clear, sound understanding, neither obscured nor enfeebled by party prejudice or personal selfishness."—*Daily News.*

"As the work of an honest able writer, these Suggestions are well worthy of attention, and no doubt they will generally be duly appreciated."—*Observer.*

British Rule in India. By Harriet Martineau.

Fifth Thousand. Price 2*s.* 6*d. cloth.*

"A good compendium of a great subject."—*National Review.*

"A succinct and comprehensive volume."—*Leader.*

Traits and Stories of Anglo-Indian Life. By Lieut.-Colonel Addison.

With Eight Illustrations, price 5*s. cloth.*

"A collection of amusing anecdotes."—*Critic.*

Tiger Shooting in India. By Lieutenant William Rice, 25th Bombay N. I.

Super Royal 8*vo. With Twelve Plates in Chroma-lithography.* 21*s. cloth.*

"These adventures, told in handsome large print, with spirited chromo-lithographs to illustrate them, make the volume before us as pleasant reading as any record of sporting achievements we have ever taken in hand."—*Athenæum.*

"A remarkably pleasant book of adventures during several seasons of 'large game' hunting in Rajpootana. The twelve chromolithographs are very valuable accessories to the narrative; they have wonderful spirit and freshness."—*Globe.*

The Commerce of India with Europe, and its Political Effects. By B. A. Irving, Esq., Author of "The Theory and Practice of Caste."

Post 8*vo, price* 7*s.* 6*d. cloth.*

Views and Opinions of Brigadier-General Jacob, C.B. Collected and Edited by Captain Lewis Pelly, Late Political Secretary Persian Expeditionary Force.

Demy 8*vo, price* 12*s. cloth.*

Papers of the late Lord Metcalfe. Selected and Edited by J. W. Kaye.

Demy 8*vo, price* 16*s. cloth.*

The Life of Mahomet and History of Islam to the Era of the Hegira. By William Muir, Esq., Bengal Civil Service.

Two Volumes 8*vo, price* 32*s. cloth.*

WORKS ON INDIA AND THE EAST—*continued.*

Tracts on the Native Army of India. By Brigadier-General JACOB, C.B.

8vo, price 2s. 6d.

Rifle Practice. By Brigadier-General JACOB, C.B.

Fourth Edition, 8vo, price 2s.

The English in Western India; being the Early History of the Factory at Surat, of Bombay. By PHILIP ANDERSON, A.M.

Second Edition, 8vo, price 14s. cloth.

Life in Ancient India. By MRS. SPEIR.

With Sixty Illustrations by G. SCHARF. *8vo, price 15s., elegantly bound in cloth, gilt edges.*

The Cauvery, Kistnah, and Godavery: being a Report on the Works constructed on those Rivers, for the Irrigation of Provinces in the Presidency of Madras. By R. BAIRD SMITH, F.G.S., Lt.-Col. Bengal Engineers, &c., &c.

In demy 8vo, with 19 Plans, price 28s. cloth.

The Bhilsa Topes; or, Budhist Monuments of Central India. By MAJOR CUNNINGHAM.

One Volume, 8vo, with Thirty-three Plates, price 30s. cloth.

The Chinese and their Rebellions. By THOMAS TAYLOR MEADOWS.

One Thick Volume, 8vo, with Maps, price 18s. cloth.

On the Culture and Commerce of Cotton in India. By Dr. FORBES ROYLE. *8vo, price 18s. cloth.*

The Fibrous Plants of India fitted for Cordage, Clothing, and Paper. By Dr. FORBES ROYLE. *8vo, price 12s. cloth.*

The Productive Resources of India. By Dr. FORBES ROYLE. Super Royal 8vo, price 14s. cloth.

Royle's Review of the Measures adopted in India for the Improved Culture of Cotton. 8vo, 2s. 6d. *cloth.*

WORKS ON INDIA AND THE EAST.—*continued.*

A Sketch of Assam; with some Account of the Hill Tribes. Coloured Plates, 8vo, price 14*s.* cloth.

Butler's Travels and Adventures in Assam. One Volume 8vo, with Plates, price 12*s.* cloth.

Dr. Wilson on Infanticide in Western India. Demy 8vo, price 12*s.*

Rev. James Coley's Journal of the Sutlej Campaign. Fcap. 8vo, price 4*s.* cloth.

Crawfurd's Grammar and Dictionary of the Malay Language. 2 vols. 8vo, price 36*s.* cloth.

Roberts's Indian Exchange Tables. 8vo. Second Edition, enlarged, price 10*s.* 6*d.* cloth.

Waring on Abscess in the Liver. 8vo, price 3*s.* 6*d.*

Laurie's Second Burmese War—Rangoon. Post 8vo, with Plates, price 10*s.* 6*d.* cloth.

Laurie's Pegu. Post 8vo, price 14*s.* cloth.

Boyd's Turkish Interpreter: a Grammar of the Turkish Language. 8vo, price 12*s.*

Bridgnell's Indian Commercial Tables. Royal 8vo, price 21*s.*, half-bound.

The Bombay Quarterly Review. Nos. 1 to 9 at 5*s.* 10 to 13, price 6*s.* each.

Baillie's Land Tax of India. According to the Moohummudan Law. 8vo, price 6*s.* cloth.

Baillie's Moohummudan Law of Sale. 8vo, price 14*s.* cloth.

Irving's Theory and Practice of Caste. 8vo, price 5*s.* cloth.

Gingell's Ceremonial Usages of the Chinese. Imperial 8vo, price 9*s.* cloth.

NEW NOVELS.

(TO BE HAD AT ALL LIBRARIES).

Eva Desmond; or, Mutation. 3 vols. (*Now ready.*)

My Lady: a Tale of Modern Life. 2 vols. (*Just ready.*)

Maud Skillicorne's Penance. By MARY CATHERINE JACKSON, Author of "The Story of My Wardship." 2 vols.

"The style is natural, and displays considerable dramatic power."—*Critic.*

The Cruelest Wrong of All. By the Author of "Margaret; or, Prejudice at Home." 1 vol.

"It has the first requisite of a work of fiction—it is amusing."—*Globe.*

The Moors and the Fens. By F. G. TRAFFORD. 3 vols.

"The plot is unhackneyed, and the composition is particularly good."—*Critic.*

"The plot is natural, and skilfully worked out; many of the scenes are described with great power, and the characters look like portraits from life."—*Ladies' Newspaper.*

Gaston Bligh. By L. S. LAVENU, Author of "Erlesmere." 2 vols.

The Three Chances. By the Author of "The Fair Carew." 3 vols.

The White House by the Sea: a Love Story. By M. BETHAM-EDWARDS. 2 vols.

Riverston. By GEORGIANA M. CRAIK. 3 vols.

The Professor. By CURRER BELL. 2 vols.

The Noble Traytour. A Chronicle. 3 vols.

Farina; a Legend of Cologne. By GEORGE MEREDITH. 1 vol.

Below the Surface: a Story of English Country Life. 3 vols.

The Roua Pass; or, Englishmen in the Highlands. By ERICK MACKENZIE. 3 vols.

Kathie Brande. By HOLME LEE. 2 vols.

Friends of Bohemia; or, Phases of London Life. By E. M. WHITTY, Author of "The Governing Classes." 2 vols.

Lucian Playfair. By THOMAS MACKERN. 3 vols.

NOVELS FORTHCOMING.

Sylvan Holt's Daughter. By Holme Lee, Author of "Kathie Brande," &c. 3 vols. (*Nearly ready.*)

Lost and Won. By Georgiana M. Craik, Author of "Riverston." 1 vol.

An Old Debt. By Florence Dawson. 2 vols.

Old and Young. 1 vol.

A New Novel. By the Author of "Amberhill." 3 vols.

A New Novel. By the Author of "Tales of the Bush," &c. 3 vols.

NEW BOOKS FOR YOUNG READERS.

By the Author of "Round the Fire," &c.

Old Gingerbread and the School-boys.
With Four Coloured Plates. Price 3s. cloth. (*Now Ready.*)

Unica: a Story for Sunday.
With Four Cuts. Price 3s. cloth. (*Now Ready.*)

Willie's Birthday; showing how a Little Boy did what he Liked, and how he Enjoyed it.
With Four Illustrations. Price 2s. 6d., cloth

Willie's Rest: a Sunday Story.
With Four Illustrations. Price 2s. 6d. cloth.

"Graceful little tales, containing some pretty parables, and a good deal of simple feeling."—*Economist.*

"Extremely well written story books, amusing and moral, and got up in a very handsome style."—*Morning Herald.*

Uncle Jack, the Fault Killer.
With Four Illustrations. Price 3s. cloth.

"An excellent little book of moral improvement made pleasant to children; it is far beyond the common-place moral tale in design and execution."—*Globe.*

Round the Fire: Six Stories for Young Readers.
Square 16mo, with Four Illustrations, price 3s. cloth.

"Charmingly written tales for the young."—*Leader.*

"Six delightful little stories."—*Guardian.*

"Simple and very interesting."—*National Review.*

"True children's stories."—*Athenæum.*

The King of the Golden River; or, the Black Brothers. By John Ruskin, M.A.
Third Edition, with 22 Illustrations by Richard Doyle. *Price 2s. 6d.*

"This little fancy tale is by a master-hand. The story has a charming moral."—*Examiner.*

Rhymes for Little Ones.
With numerous Cuts. Price 1s. 6d. cloth.

MISCELLANEOUS.

Sir John Herschel's Astronomical Observations made at the Cape of Good Hope. 4to, with plates, price 4*l.* 4*s.* cloth.

Darwin's Geological Observations on Coral Reefs, Volcanic Islands, and on South America. With maps, plates, and woodcuts, 10*s.* 6*d.* cloth.

Levi's Commercial Law of the World. Two Vols., royal 4to, price 6*l.* cloth.

Playford's Hints for Investing Money. Second Edition, post 8vo, price 2*s.* 6*d.* cloth.

Sir John Forbes's Memorandums in Ireland. Two Vols., post 8vo, price 1*l.* 1*s.* cloth.

Leigh Hunt's Men, Women, and Books. Two Vols. Price 10*s.* cloth.

——— *Table Talk.* 3*s.* 6*d.* cloth.

——— *Wit and Humour.* 5*s.* cloth.

——— *Jar of Honey.* 5*s.* cloth.

Juvenile Delinquency. By M. Hill and C. F. Cornwallis. Post 8vo, price 6*s.* cloth.

Doubleday's True Law of Population. Third Edition, 8vo, 10*s.* cloth.

McCann's Argentine Provinces, &c. Two Vols., post 8vo, with illustrations, price 24*s.* cloth.

Goethe's Conversations with Eckermann. Translated by John Oxenford. Two Vols., post 8vo, 10*s.* cloth.

Kavanagh's Women of Christianity Exemplary for Piety and Charity. Post 8vo, with Portraits, price 12*s.*, in embossed cloth, gilt edges.

Elementary Works on Social Economy. Uniform in foolscap 8vo, half-bound.

I.—OUTLINES OF SOCIAL ECONOMY. 1*s.* 6*d.*
II.—PROGRESSIVE LESSONS IN SOCIAL SCIENCE.
III.—INTRODUCTION TO THE SOCIAL SCIENCES. 2*s.*
IV.—OUTLINES OF THE UNDERSTANDING. 2*s.*
V.—WHAT AM I? WHERE AM I? WHAT OUGHT I TO DO? &c. 1*s.* sewed.

Swainson's Lectures on New Zealand. Crown 8vo, price 2*s.* 6*d.* cloth.

Swainson's Account of Auckland. Post 8vo, with a View, price 6*s.* cloth.

POETRY.

The Six Legends of King Goldenstar. By the late ANNA BRADSTREET. Fcap. 8vo, price 5*s.*

"The author evinces more than ordinary power, a vivid imagination, guided by a mind of lofty aim."—*Globe.*

England in Time of War. By SYDNEY DOBELL, Author of "Balder," "The Roman," &c. Crown 8vo, 5*s.* cloth.

"That Mr. Dobell is a poet, 'England in time of War' bears witness in many single lines, and in two or three short poems."—*Athenæum.*

The Cruel Sister, AND OTHER POEMS. Fcap. 8vo, 4*s.* cl.

"There are traces of power, and the versification displays freedom and skill."—*Guardian.*

Poems of Past Years. By Sir ARTHUR HALLAM ELTON, Bart., M.P. Fcap. 8vo, 3*s.* cloth.

"A refined, scholarly, and gentlemanly mind is apparent all through this volume."—*Leader.*

Poems. By Mrs. FRANK P. FELLOWS. Fcap. 8vo, 3*s.* cl.

"There is easy simplicity in the diction, and elegant naturalness in the thought."—*Spectator.*

Poetry from Life. By C. M. K. Fcap. 8vo, cl. gilt, 5*s.*

"Elegant verses. The author has a pleasing fancy and a refined mind."—*Economist.*

Poems. By WALTER R. CASSELS. Fcap. 8vo, price 3*s.* 6*d.* cloth.

"Mr. Cassels has deep poetical feeling, and gives promise of real excellence. His poems are written sometimes with a strength of expression by no means common."—*Guardian.*

Garlands of Verse. By THOMAS LEIGH. Fcap. 8vo, price 5*s.* cloth.

"One of the best things in the 'Garlands of Verse' is an Ode to Toil. There, as elsewhere, there is excellent feeling."—*Examiner.*

Balder. By SYDNEY DOBELL. Crown 8vo, 7*s.* 6*d.* cloth.

"The writer has fine qualities; his level of thought is lofty, and his passion for the beautiful has the truth of instinct."—*Athenæum.*

Poems. By WILLIAM BELL SCOTT. Fcap. 8vo, 5*s.* cl.

"Mr. Scott has poetical feeling, keen observation, deep thought, and command of language."—*Spectator.*

Poems. By MARY MAYNARD. Fcap. 8vo, 4*s.* cloth.

"We have rarely met with a volume of poems displaying so large an amount of power, blended with so much delicacy of feeling and grace of expression."—*Church of England Quarterly.*

Poems. By CURRER, ELLIS, and ACTON BELL. Fcap. 8vo, 4*s.* cloth.

Select Odes of Horace. In English Lyrics. By J. T. BLACK. Fcap. 8vo, price 4*s.* cloth.

"Rendered into English Lyrics with a vigour and heartiness rarely, if ever, surpassed."—*Critic.*